mentors

and

supervisors

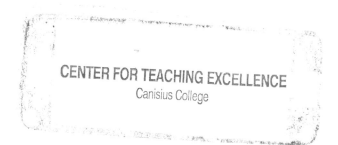

mentors and supervisors

Nathalie Friedman, Ph.D.

Columbia University

A Report Prepared for the Institute of International
Education

June 1987

TABLE OF CONTENTS

Foreword 1

Chapter 1: Introduction 5

Chapter 2 : The Choice of a University 18

Chapter 3: The Predissertation Years 24

Chapter 4: The Choice of an Advisor..34

Chapter 5: A Researchable Topic..45

Chapter 6: Mentors and Supervisors 56

Chapter 7: Students as Advisors:
Mutual Advising Among Peers.................................87

Chapter 8: Foreign and American Doctoral Students: 96
Conclusions and Recommendations

Appendix: The Foreign Student Office 102

References 106

Foreword

Americans, as Tocqueville taught us, despise inequality. In most contexts this seems a virtuous characteristic. The love of equality is a dynamic and positive force in our society, motivating and justifying social change that uproots inequality, seen as a preeminent form of injustice. However, there is also a pathological element in extreme egalitarianism, a pathology which, for example, permits uncritical parents to neglect their responsibility for discipline, or which inhibits us from the proper exercise of authority. This pathology may manifest itself as a failure to distinguish legitimate from illegitimate forms of inequality. Superiorities of age and experience or of taste and education are not accepted because they appear—in a calamitous confusion—to belong to the same class as racial or gender superiority. Another manifestation of this pathology is in the despising of the unequal and an unconscious loathing of the fawning, flattering, obsequious conduct that seems to arise naturally where the premise of inequality seems as inevitable as does the premise of equality to Americans.

The relatively benign forms of this pathology are familiar to every university professor. American students press steadily, for reasons they usually cannot consciously articulate, toward relations of equality with their teachers. We come to recognize this pressure initially in the troublesome issue of "first names." Should a student address a professor by his or her given name? Most of us answer this question with a host of other questions: How old is the student? How advanced is the student? How old is the professor? How

1

closely involved are they in research? The usual presumption is that there is some right set of answers that qualify a student to use the professor's first name in addressing him or her. Few American academic people today would utterly deny the propriety of this level of equality for some students at some stages of their work. We have difficulty managing the intimacy normal to research supervision within the formally hierarchical professor-student relationship.

There are few societies outside of North America where it is thought proper for students to address professors by their first names. American practice in this regard is quite peculiar and difficult to interpret without the perspective needed to see it as a problem intrinsic to the version of radical egalitarianism developed in American culture. (Students in other ideologically egalitarian societies, such as the U.S.S.R. and the People's Republic of China, do not address professors by their first names; classlessness and the obliteration of all social distinctions are not confused with one another.) Thus, the awkwardnesses created by this apparently simple practice can be assumed to affect foreign students generally. The issue of the use of first names is a relatively trivial one, but it is a symptom of a pervasive difficulty faced by foreign graduate students in American universities. I raise it here as a way of opening up the entire range of issues affecting the relationship between graduate students and their faculty supervisors from an angle of vision that avoids the usual considerations of academic ability and finances.

Nathalie Friedman's fascinating study of the relations between foreign graduate students and their American dissertation advisors opens up a great many of these subtle problems, the ones that are not so often cited as impediments to success in doctoral programs because they are difficult to name and describe. Her study is based on an investigation carried out with good judgment and an imaginative method adapted to restricted time and limited financial support. Most readers will want to know what differences might have been seen if other disciplines or if universities in other regions of the U.S. were included in the study. Perhaps that larger study is waiting to be done, but in the meantime there is much in this one that will enrich our understanding and sensitize us to the special needs and expectations of foreign doctoral students, such as the predissertation students from Chile who feel that their status is diminished in American universities, and the Lebanese students who feel a lack of Mediterranean warmth and true intimacy in their American advisors.

Since I am an anthropologist and I have done most of my research for over 25 years in India, I have had more to do with Indian, Bangladeshi, and other Asian students than I have with students from other world areas. It is natural that my attention should turn to the problems of hierarchical social relations and American egalitarianism. However, there is a great deal more in this study that deserves close attention. It is tempting to go through the rich collection of quoted testimony, selecting evidence in support of one's pet theories about foreign students in America. We would all do best, however, to study all of the evidence and see the full range of variation before moving to conclusions about particular difficulties. The problems are far from uniform across fields and institutions, not to say across groups of graduate students from different cultural and linguistic areas.

Dr. Friedman's chapter on "Mentors and Advisors" offers several challenges to those of us who regularly—I am tempted to say "habitually"—guide foreign doctoral students. Rarely does any student appear with whom we can enjoy that mutual and mutually rewarding relationship which she describes as "mentorship." Such a student is often so much like one's own self in intellectual concerns, temperament, and perhaps many other significant characteristics as well, that it becomes possible for us to identify his or her work with our own, and to derive from its success the deepest personal gratification. Most students cannot, and probably should not, be so close to their dissertation supervisors. Yet, they too need the support and sympathetic understanding that mentorship provides. Meeting one's former student in his or her home country especially after the student has become established as a faculty

3

member in a university there, can be embarrassing. To hear oneself described in terms that ought to be reserved for the true mentor is as difficult to accept as is obsequiousness in the graduate student. However, correctly understood, this experience should tell us that there is a reasonable substitute for the fully fledged mentoring relation that can provide the foreign graduate student with a very gratifying memory of doctoral work in the United States. Dr. Friedman's research offers excellent guidance on how to attain that kind of relationship even in the absence of full mutuality.

This study offers the means for graduate teachers across the gamut of academic disciplines to sharpen their sensitivities in dealing with foreign doctoral students. I encourage my colleagues to read it with minds open to the full range of testimony and interpretation it offers.

Ralph W. Nicholas
Dean of the College
The University of Chicago

1
Introduction

The Problem

The purpose of this research is to explore the nature and meaning of advising at the Ph. D. level and the conditions under which the two parties in the relationship — sponsor and advisee __ are more and less satisfied. The study focuses on the special problems experienced by foreign students when they are advisees, as compared to American students.

The years that students spend in graduate school, striving to move from the status of neophyte to that of professional, are known to be fraught with difficulty, strain and frustration. Graduate students must overcome a series of obstacles and undergo a number of trials along the way to the doctoral or professional degree. They must complete a specified number of credits and take increasingly difficult and advanced courses. They must fulfill various foreign language and/or mathematics requirements and pass a variety of written and oral examinations. They must propose a thesis topic, obtain a faculty sponsor, prepare and defend a dissertation proposal, and write and defend the dissertation. Further, many must make considerable financial sacrifices in order to obtain their degrees, suffering the kind of penury that has become legendary as part and parcel of the graduate experience.

In other respects as well, the role of the aspiring professional during the graduate years is not easy. Students must maintain a rather precarious balance between subservience and independence. On the one hand, the graduate student is expected and encouraged to think critically, to analyze the facts at hand, to ask penetrating questions, and to make independent judgments and decisions. On the other hand, students recognize that it may be dangerous to reject the intellectual approach or authority of faculty members because these are the persons who evaluate their work and who serve as gate-keepers to the professional world they are seeking to enter. Further, it has been suggested (Rosen and Bates, 1967) that even the teaching assistantship, as vigorously as it is sought and as valuable an experience as it may be, can provide considerable opportunity for role strain as students are forced to shift back and forth from a position of authority (over undergraduates) to one of subordination (to faculty).

There is a fairly impressive body of literature on the general subject of graduate student socialization, particularly on the socialization of pre-professionals. The research in this area touches on such themes as how entrants learn to become graduate students (e.g. Becker, et al., 1961; Bess, 1978; LeBaron, 1982; Merton, et al., 1957; Turow, 1977); the stresses and strains of the graduate years (e.g. Loewenberg, 1969; Madrey, 1983; Nelson, 1959; Valdez, 1982); how neophytes come to view themselves as professionals (e.g. Gottlieb, 1961; Light, 1980; Persell, 1976); how faculty see their roles vis-`a-vis students (e.g. Berelson, 1960; Turner, 1972); and how mentors can shape careers in very concrete ways (e.g. Alleman, et al., 1984; Stein, 1981; Zuckerman, 1977).

As compared to the process of socialization, little is known about the period of graduate or professional education during which the student, having completed course and examination requirements, is engaged in the process of writing the thesis or dissertation. This period in the life of the graduate student, which may take a minimum of two years but more often extends over four or more years, is a virtual unknown but for anecdotal accounts. Students in these difficult years are well described by a young campus journalist (Lafferty, 1986):

They dread the fact that they must get started, and they dread the thought of completion. They feel guilty about not spending time with their family and friends while in the midst of research, and guilty about spending time with loved ones when they should be doing research. They hate working as waitresses and taxi drivers to earn money, and fear they may not find anything better when it's all over. They feel overwhelmed by their task, nervous about their abilities, isolated by their problems. They are graduate students researching and writing their doctoral dissertation.

It is curious that so little is known about the dissertation years for evidence has accumulated over the past several decades indicating that the highest hurdle of the doctoral program is the completion of the thesis or dissertation. Both students and faculty agree that the dissertation is the most difficult requirement of the doctoral program, and that writing a dissertation is a stressful and frustrating experience for many students (Heiss, 1967; Madrey, 1983; Page, 1959; Strom, 1965). The term "A.B.D." ("All But the Dissertation") has become a commonplace — in fact, it is estimated that approximately one third of those who complete the course requirements for the doctoral degree fail to complete the dissertation itself.

At question are the reasons for this high attrition rate. Research on the subject is sparse, but what does exist suggests that neither financial difficulties nor lack of academic ability adequately explain why the dissertation is often not completed. For example, Berelson (1960) found that while seven out of ten graduate deans cited lack of financial resources as a major reason for students not completing the doctoral program, fewer than one in four students cited this as the critical factor. Berelson suggests that while money may indeed be the official reason students give to the deans, in reality there are other factors that account for failing to complete the dissertation. In his words: "What is frankness between doctoral candidates becomes in the dean's office lack of funds or a personal change in plans."

Turner (1972) reviews a body of literature on the subject of doctoral attrition and concludes that lack of academic ability is not a crucial factor. She notes that studies comparing those who obtained the degree and those who completed all the requirements except the dissertation, (e.g., Wright, 1964, Renetzky, 1966) failed to find differences between the two groups on such measures as I.Q., performance on the Graduate Record Examination, or scholastic average in the Master of Arts degree program. Some of the studies reviewed by Turner found that psychological factors, such as motivation, ego strength, and emotional maturity, differentiated successful and unsuccessful graduate students (e.g., Friedenberg and Roth, 1954; Nelson, 1959; Strom, 1965).

Among the non-substantive factors contributing to failure to complete the dissertation, the quality of the thesis advisor/student relationship may be particularly important, according to Turner. One study she examined found that frequency of contact between student and sponsor was related to length of time required to complete the dissertation (Rosenhaupt, 1958). Another indicated that A.B.D's showed considerably less ability than degree recipients to achieve a cooperative, working relationship with the thesis advisor (Renetzky, 1966). Further, several studies from the 1950s and 1960s found substantial student dissatisfaction with the amount of time available for consultation with faculty advisors (e.g. Doty, 1962; Irwin, 1960; Kishkunas, 1958). In a more recent study of twenty-five A.B.D's (Jacks, et al., 1983), eleven (44 percent) cited a poor working relationship with the advisor as a reason for failing to complete the thesis. This factor was cited by more students than was any other, with the exception of financial difficulties, also cited by eleven A.B.D's.

Turner (1972) found a lack of agreement among faculty as well as between faculty and students about the proper role of the advisor, that is, about such matters as how involved the advisor should be in the selection of the dissertation topic, how available an advisor should be to students, or whether a professor has the right to refuse to serve as a thesis advisor.

While the lack of clarity about the norms governing the advisor/advisee relationship may ultimately be only one factor in the high doctoral attrition rate, it is very possible the relationship that a student establishes with the dissertation or thesis advisor affects not only the quality of the dissertation and the length of time it takes to complete it, but also the amount of stress and strain for both parties — student and advisor — during this period. And the literature tells us virtually nothing about this relationship, that is, about the nature of advising at the doctoral level, about the norms and expectations governing the advisor-advisee situation, or about the conditions under which the two parties are more and less likely to attain their objectives.

Although the dissertation years in general, and the sponsor-student relationship in particular, may be stressful and trying for most graduate students, there is reason to suspect these years may present special problems for foreign graduate students. The latter, who comprise more than 41.4 percent of full-time graduate enrollments (Open Doors, 1985/86), are likely to arrive with well-formed expectations about graduate study and about student-faculty relations, based on experience in their home country. Further, their financial situation may be even more precarious than that of American students, particularly as they are usually constrained from holding off-campus jobs and they are less likely to be able to draw upon a pool of relatives and friends for emotional, social, and financial support. Because student-faculty relationships in some countries may be more formal and, in others, less formal than in America, foreign students may find themselves uncertain about how to relate to their thesis advisors. Thus, students from some countries may be accustomed to stringent supervision from faculty advisors and thus may be seen by American faculty as overly dependent. In other cases, students who enjoyed an informal relationship with faculty in the home country may be regarded as arrogant and overly demanding by American thesis advisors. In addition, lack of facility with the English language may be a constraining factor, both academically and socially, as they attempt to interact with fellow students and faculty.

The focus of this report, accordingly, is on the advisor-advisee relationship at the doctoral level with particular emphasis on how this relationship works for the foreign student. What, for example, is the content of the advising relationship? Is it functionally specific, in that it focuses on the teaching and learning of the substance of a discipline or the execution of a specific piece of research? Do students see their advisors, and do advisors see themselves, as more than agents to expedite completion of a thesis? Are they perceived as mentors, that is, role models, scholars with whom to identify, protectors, enhancers of professional advancement? Are they looked to for advice and assistance on more than academic matters, for example, career or personal problems? Do some advisor-advisee relationships gradually evolve beyond the traditional boundaries of teacher and student into a collegial, collaborative one? Do structural factors, such as the size and quality of departments, the availability of research monies, or the state of the job market for graduates in certain fields, play a role in the advising process? And finally, are the answers to these questions different when the advisee is a foreign rather than an American student?

These are some of the questions that this paper addresses, in the hope that illumination of the advising process will be helpful to all participants by creating greater awareness of potential problems and pitfalls. It is particularly hoped that identifying the special implications for foreign graduate students will make it possible to provide informed and realistic guidance to these students as they prepare to embark on doctoral study.

Methodology

As noted above, this research focuses on the doctoral advising process with special emphasis on how this process may present special problems for the foreign graduate student. The thrust of the study is primarily exploratory. There is only scant literature on the subject of graduate advising and even less on the advising of foreign graduate students. Accordingly, the research employs a detailed case study approach — an approach which enables the researcher to identify many of the important issues in a hitherto unexplored area through detailed probing in semi-structured focused interviews. At the same time, sufficient numbers of advisors and advisees have been interviewed to permit at least some comparisons of attitudes and experiences, both between advisors and students, and between American and foreign students. Nevertheless, we must emphasize that a study such as this has only limited generalizability, given the small number of institutions and of students that have been examined.

The Research Sites

The study sites are six graduate departments selected to yield as comprehensive as possible an understanding of this relatively unchartered area. Specifically, the case studies were conducted in six graduate departments of four universities in a major metropolitan area in the Northeast. The rationale for selecting the fields of study in which advising was being carried out was based on the hypothesis that relations between students and faculty might vary from field to field depending on, for example, the availability of research monies and the extent to which research relating to the thesis is carried out by groups of people or individually. The natural sciences or engineering tend to command large research funds and research is often carried out in groups. In the humanities, by contrast, research monies play almost no role and the individualized research process is likely to be a very lonely one. The social sciences tend to fall between these two extremes.

Accordingly, the three fields or disciplines selected for study were engineering, economics, and history, as representative of the sciences, the social sciences, and the humanities respectively. Engineering was selected primarily because very large proportions of the graduate students in this field come from foreign countries. In fact, at many universities, foreign engineering graduate students substantially outnumber those who are U.S.-born. Among the social sciences, economics has the largest number of foreign graduate students, as is the case for history in the humanities.

For each of these fields, we selected two departments in which to conduct the interviews with advisors and students. As much as possible, we tried to vary the size and quality of the departments. It was hypothesized that the process of matching advisor and advisee in large departments might be more universalistic and in small ones more particularistic, thus affecting the quality of the relationships. Similarly, in high-quality departments we would expect greater sophistication on the part of graduate students in their selection of faculty advisors. At the same time, faculty with high prestige — "stars" — often have heavy demands on their time from many sources with little time left for advising graduate students. In departments of less high quality the opposite obtains, and the factors conducive to positive or negative relationships may vary accordingly. Given the small number of departments studied, it was not, of course, possible to carry out rigorous contextual analysis of the advisor-advisee relationship. Yet, as Table 1 indicates, the departments do vary sufficiently in size and quality to allow for the study of this relationship under varying conditions.

TABLE 1

Departments	Number of Ph.D. candidates*	Quality rating*	Number of Interviews	
			Advisors	Students
Electrical engineering				
1	56	3.6	2	6
2	159	1.8	2	4
Economics				
1	213	4.3	2	6
2	82	3.2	3	6
History				
1	305	4.5	2	6
2	60	3.1	2	5

*Jones, et al. (eds.) An Assessment of Research Doctorate Programs in the United States. Washington, D.C.: National Academy Press, 1982.

The Sample

In each of the six departments, we first interviewed the chairperson to obtain his perceptions about the way in which the advising process operates in that department, as well as to obtain the names of at least two professors who were, as far as the chairperson knew, currently advising both American and foreign students. As Table 1 indicates, we then interviewed two or three faculty advisors from each of the departments and then two or three of each sponsor's advisees. As far as was possible, we interviewed one American and two foreign advisees of each sponsor.

In addition, at each of the four universities we spoke with an administrator in the office for foreign student affairs to obtain a picture of the foreign student population and of that university's policies and procedures for advising and counseling foreign students. At two of the four universities we also spoke with a Dean of Graduate Studies. Altogether, 58 persons were interviewed:

Directors of Foreign Student Affairs	4
Graduate deans	2
Departmental chairpersons	6
Advisors	13
Students	
Foreign	22
American	11
TOTAL	58

The foreign students who were interviewed came from a total of fifteen countries: three came from East Asia (Korea and the People's Republic of China); four from South and Southeast Asia (India, Pakistan, Malaysia); five were from the Middle East (Iran, Israel, and Lebanon); four came from European countries (Greece, Poland, Portugal, and Sweden), and six were from Latin America and the Caribbean (Argentina, Chile, Cuba, Jamaica, and Mexico).

The average age of the students interviewed was 33. It should be noted, however, that the American students were some-what younger than their foreign counterparts (30 compared to 35). Despite their relative youth, one-half of the American students, but only one out of three of the foreign students, were married at the time they were writing their dissertations. Further, the socioeconomic background of American and foreign students differed substantially. American students were far more likely than foreign students to report that their parents — both mother and father —were college graduates or better. In fact, this was the case for all except two American respondents, but for only a handful of foreign students. Parents of American students were, or had been, engaged in such occupations as college professor, physician, clergyman, engineer, or librarian. In contrast, only three foreign students reported that their mothers had received any education beyond high school and, in several cases one or both parents of foreign students were illiterate. Almost all happened to come from working-class back-grounds with the exception of the few who reported that their fathers were merchants or businessmen. It should be noted that this is not typical of the foreign student population. Most foreign students, according to previous research, tend to come from upper- or middle-class families. (See, for example, L. Solmon and B. Young, The Foreign Student Factor, IIE, 1987.)

The Interview

Interviews with faculty advisors averaged one hour or more in length and addressed the following areas:

1. The selection process, e.g.: how they select or are selected by advisees; how many advisees, on the average, they have each year; relationship of the selection process to the availability of research monies.

2. The dissertation topic, e.g.: respective roles of advisor and advisee in selecting a topic; the process of narrowing down a topic.

3. Types of guidance requested and given, e.g.: academic; career; personal.

4. Expectations vs. experience regarding e.g.: amount and type of assistance; amount of time; nature of the relationship.

5. Description of particularly "successful" and the opposite, particularly disastrous, encounters.

6. Perceived differences between American and foreign graduate students, e.g.: special problems or strengths of foreign students; variations by country of origin.

7. Background characteristics.

Interviews with graduate students were generally between one and one and one-half hours in length, although several were as long as two and one-half hours. They covered much the same areas as those with faculty but, in addition, information was obtained on:

1. How the student came to attend the particular university, school, or department.

2. General level of satisfaction with courses, faculty, department, scope of academic options.

3. For foreign students, the extent to which expectations were structured by relationships with faculty in home country.

4. Extent of mutual advising among students.

5. Future plans (educational, occupational, residential), concerns about job prospects, expectations regarding continued relationship with advisor after completion of degree.

While it was sometimes a difficult and time-consuming process to schedule appointments with busy faculty advisors, none actually declined to be interviewed. Most, as a matter of fact, expressed great interest in the subject of possible differences in advising American and foreign doctoral students. As one put it:

> You know, I've never stopped to think about that in any serious
> way — and it's true that there are differences.

Nor did any students refuse to be interviewed. For many, whether American or foreign, the opportunity to talk about the problems, tensions, and anomie at the dissertation stage was a welcome one. In fact, the interview itself seemed to constitute a cathartic experience, as students spoke — occasionally with anger and resentment, sometimes with genuine pleasure and satisfaction

— about what to them was clearly a salient issue: the relationship with their thesis advisor. We turn now to what they and their advisors had to say about this relationship.

Just one methodological note: This study was not designed to permit generalization to the graduate student or faculty population as a whole, nor to the foreign graduate student population. Such generalization would require a far larger sample and substantially greater rigor in selecting both research sites and respondents. The purpose of the research was rather to uncover patterns, relationships, and critical variables that might provide a deeper understanding of the ways in which advising relationships are initiated and carried on. Such understanding, in turn, may serve to suggest intervention strategies that will provide better orientation and guidance to graduate students, particularly those who have come from foreign countries to study at American universities.

2
The Choice of
a University

What were the factors which led students, particularly foreign students, to choose a given university for graduate study? The question is a significant one because students who choose to attend a university specifically to write a dissertation under the aegis of a particular professor are likely to develop a relationship with that professor that is far different from that of a student who comes to the university for other, particularly non-academic, reasons.

From an academic perspective, there is probably an ideal script that narrates the student's odyssey from college to graduate school: During the undergraduate years the student became interested in a given subject, perhaps wrote a senior thesis on that subject and decided to pursue study in that area at the graduate level. S/he had read books or articles by Professor X and perhaps had even met Professor X when he came to the university as a guest lecturer. So the student decided to apply to the university at which Professor X teaches and hoped to write the dissertation under the sponsorship of Professor X. All works out well. The student is accepted, takes courses with his future mentor, perhaps TA's for him, and eventually writes the thesis under his sponsorship.

Only three or four of the thirty-five graduate students interviewed had followed the above script. In just a few cases were the reasons for attending a particular university directly related to the desire to study with, or work under, a given professor or in a particularly strong department. An American student in a highly rated history department was one of these few exceptions:

> I was originally in an MA/Ph.D. program at another university but was unhappy with the intellectual approach there. I was not being taught how to do practical research. My advisor was teaching a course there at the time and I had a chance to meet and talk with him. I decided that I'd like to study with him. Then I went to the rankings book and it looked as if this university really was the best in my field so I decided to come here. I always knew that I wanted to work with R (advisor).

Another American student in the same discipline but at another university had been advised by her undergraduate "mentor" to go there because of the presence of a particular professor:

> I had heard of this professor, so I took my mentor's advice and came there. It's funny though — I ended up not working with him because I took a few courses with him and found that his teaching style bothered me. He wasn't receptive to students' ideas. On the other hand, I liked the freedom of expression that S (advisor) provided and decided to work with him.

A Chinese student in the same department had transferred from a graduate program at a smaller university specifically to study with the professor who became his thesis sponsor:

> She's an authority in my field and I decided that was whom I wanted to work with. In fact, I got in touch with her before I transferred and she agreed to be my advisor.

Several students said they had chosen to study at a particular university because they had heard it had a fine reputation or because they had used textbooks written by a professor from that university.

An engineering student said:

> I had read textbooks written by professors here and I thought they were good. So I applied.

American students were far more likely than foreign students to have had the advice of an undergraduate professor, generally a senior thesis advisor with whom they had established a close relationship. Only a few foreign students, notably from Latin America, had had the benefit of such advice. A Chilean student, in a select history department said:

> I came here because I knew that the department was very strong. How did I know? It's known all over the world. All my undergraduate professors at home had MA's and PhD's from the United States, so they knew the rankings of the various schools.

But then he added:

> Also — I wanted to be in the Northeast. I thought that it would be more interesting than some place in the Midwest or the South.

For the majority of students, whether American or foreign, the decision to attend a particular university was based far less on academic or intellectual than on financial, geographical, or other practical concerns. Two American engineering students, for example, had been undergraduates at their respective institutions and had decided to stay on. Said one:

> I felt comfortable in the department and they said that I could most probably have an assistantship. So I decided to stay right here.

And the other:

> When I finished college, I didn't really know what I wanted to do.

My father, who teaches in the department here, suggested that I try staying on for the Masters. I liked it and I was able to get an RAship so I'm still here.

Foreign students, in particular, were motivated less by intellectual than by financial and geographic factors. A young woman from Spain explained:

My husband was able to get a job in this area so I was basically limited to two schools that had graduate programs in my field. I applied to both but this department gave me money and it involved less commuting.

And a student from Greece:

I wanted to be in this part of the country and I got a good financial deal here. Fortunately, it's a pretty good department.

Geographical concerns were particularly salient for a Chinese student who explained how he happened to come to this particular university:

I had been studying in Texas and I really wanted to see the northern part of the country, especially around this area where I was told it wouldn't be too cold. So I just looked through the catalogues to see which schools in the area seemed to have a good engineering program.

Several students reported that essentially they had had little or no choice about where to study. As a man from Portugal noted wryly:

This was the best offer I got— I was rejected by my first two choices!

A Latin American woman at a prestigious university said:

My senior advisor at college had warned me about this university, especially insofar as student/ faculty relations were concerned. But I had to take this — I was only wait-listed at my first-choice school.

Finally, for two foreign engineering students — one from China, the other from Lebanon — it appeared to be almost accidental that they had ended up at their respective schools. Said the student from China:

I guess you could say that it was almost an accident that I came here. I applied to many, many schools and this was the one that accepted me first, so I took it.

And the Lebanese student:

It was very much a coincidence that I ended up in this department. My sponsor in Washington, D.C. had sent me here, but not for engineering. It was to study ESL (English as a Second Language). I had asked to go to a school that was in the Northeast, but where it was not too cold. After ESL, I was supposed to go to a university in Tennessee for the Ph.D. but when I got there, I found it much too snobbish. I had liked it here when I was in the ESL program, so I applied.

Thus, students' reasons for coming to a particular university for graduate study largely had to do with financial and geographical rather than academic factors. Only in a very few instances did a student — generally an American rather than a foreign student — say that s/he had chosen to come to that university because of a department's reputation or because of a desire to work with a given professor. Foreign students were obviously less likely than Americans to have information about the reputation of a particular department or to have received advice about which professors to seek out and, perhaps, which to avoid. Their general procedure was to apply to several universities in that section of the country where they preferred to live and then to choose the one that offered them the most favorable financial package. While this was sometimes the case for American students as well, the latter were much more likely to have received advice or guidance from undergraduate mentors about the better departments in their field. Similarly, through their undergraduate advisors, the Americans were more likely to be familiar with the names of professors whose areas of specialization would make them appropriate sponsors when the time came to write the dissertation.

In a word, it would appear that American students enter graduate school with a certain advantage over foreign students. They are likely to know more about the department they are entering as well as about professors who might later serve as thesis advisors. At question is the extent to which this advantage is maintained over the years of taking courses and examinations prior to the search for a thesis advisor.

3
The Predissertation Years

Before even embarking on the dissertation, most students spend approximately two to three years taking courses and up to another year studying for orals, comprehensives, or field exams. Accordingly, before becoming professionals, would-be Ph.D's must first learn to be graduate students. As neophytes, they must find a place in the competitive structure, interact with peers, and "learn the prevailing folklore of how to cope with the agents in whose hands his fate lies for several years." (Rosen and Bates, 1967:75). During this time, the extent to which they "learn the ropes"— which courses to take and which to shun, which professors to try to get to know and which to avoid, how to study for examinations — may well affect their later experience as they seek a thesis advisor and a dissertation topic.

Further, one might expect these early years to be even more difficult and problem-laden for the foreign graduate student than for his American counterpart. After all, in most instances he has just arrived in this country; he is unfamiliar with the norms and expectations of American graduate education; he is unlikely to have friends and family for support and company and, perhaps most important, his ability to communicate in English may be severely limited. In this chapter we will see how foreign and American graduate students evaluate their courses and their professors as they look back at their experiences during the predissertation years.

Recall that the study design calls for selecting three disciplines — English, history, and economics — and for looking at each of these at two different universities, one where the department is highly rated, and the other where the rating is lower (Jones et al. 1982). Departmental quality ratings, however, are based on such factors as faculty publications, percentages of faculty with research grants, or amount of research monies — not on student evaluation of courses and/or faculty. Accordingly, it is not surprising that we find little correlation between students' feelings about their respective departments and the prestige ratings of these departments. In fact, students in the less prestigious history and economics departments seemed to be more satisfied with their courses and their professors than were students in the more highly ranked departments. An American student in the lower-ranked history department perhaps provided the clue:

> I was very satisfied with the courses and I thought that most of my professors were excellent. What I liked was that the faculty here is very supportive of its graduate students, very encouraging. I think it's because they are trying to raise the quality of both the department and the university as a whole, so they want good students and they treat them well.

A Chinese student in the same department agreed:

> I think it's a very strong program. Some courses are excellent, others not as good, but none really poor. And the faculty is very good, very helpful.

And still a third student echoed these sentiments:

> Good school, good department, good faculty. Professors were always available — you could even call them at home.

In the lower-ranked economics department as well (at the same university) students were generally positive as they spoke about their courses and their professors. An Iranian student explained why he felt satisfied as he looked back at the predissertation years:

> It's a good department with plenty of electives, so I could take whatever courses I needed to round out my knowledge. I must say that my professors were very supportive and I felt this especially during the hostage situation. They understood how I felt and they made me feel comfortable about it. In addition, I came in with terrible language problems, but they were very patient and understanding.

Note that all of these graduate students based their evaluation on more than the quality of the courses. A salient factor for them was the extent to which professors were supportive and made themselves available to students. And it was the absence of this very factor which provoked negative evaluations of the predissertation years from students in the more prestigious history and economics departments.

In the higher-ranked history department, reviews were mixed. An Israeli student was very satisfied with the quality of the courses and the level and content of the readings and, even more important she said:

> I feel that I was given an understanding of how to approach historical problems. From what I can see, it's probably better here than anywhere else.

Still, she noted:

> As an M.A. student in Israel, I had close relations with the faculty. Even now when I go back, I get the best treatment. I go to their homes and have a much closer relationship with them. The Israeli environment is very different — more natural, much less formal. It was somewhat disappointing when I didn't find that here.

Other students in that history department agreed the courses offered were generally good —"tops", said one — but several noted that the department was shrinking with insufficient faculty and not enough courses to select from. (The low teaching load, conducive to faculty productivity, may under some conditions be troublesome to students.) Said one student:

> I had very little choice. I literally have had to take just about every course they offer. The problem is that they don't bring in enough junior faculty.

Another student picked up on this theme:

> There are just too many old, tenured professors and it's difficult for us to relate to them. The young faculty that they do bring in don't stay very long, so it doesn't pay to try to develop a relationship with them. I think this is a problem in general at this university, but especially in our department.

That this was indeed not a problem limited to the history department at this university, is suggested by the comments of students in economics. Despite its very high ranking, students in this department were not particularly impressed with the quality of the course offerings. Several noted that the department was uneven depending on the particular field. Said one:

> You really see it when you're taking courses in the first and second years. In some areas, like Labor Economics and Micro-economics, the professors are well past their prime. They're just not up on the field — they can't take you to the frontier. On the other hand, they're quite strong in Macroeconomics and International Trade.

Another student complained about the paucity of courses:

> There aren't enough courses offered — not enough coverage of the field. The same courses are given year after year — no

variation. The professors are old and have gone stale.

A student from Argentina also spoke of the (advanced) age of the faculty in this department:

> Those that are younger leave. They know that they won't get tenure, so there's no incentive for them to stay. Young faculty members have no one to talk to — the old professors may have been great economists at one time, but they don't update themselves. And at the same time, they don't encourage the younger faculty to develop new courses and new ideas.

On the other hand, a student from Portugal felt that the American graduate system, at least for the first two years, was much superior to the European one:

> You get a better grounding here than in Europe. In Europe, they don't offer an overall range of courses. Here, you can study relevant subjects and you get a feeling that you're working with people who are near the frontier, who are writing fundamental papers.

But far outweighing either praise or complaints about the courses in this department, was dissatisfaction regarding faculty neglect of students. One student noted that until they pass their field exams, after completing their coursework, they are literally ignored by faculty. Another suggested that there is a general attitude on the part of both faculty and administrative staff that undervalues students, and that results in poor advisement and lack of interest in students. The same student from Portugal who had praised the quality of the course offerings had this to say as well:

> When it comes to human relations, forget it! No one cares — no one. One of the problems is that you get labelled as early as the first semester and that can be a particular problem for foreign students, because we come in with handicaps. I felt from the very beginning that my professors weren't interested in me.

A Chilean student voiced a similar feeling about faculty neglect and he compared the situation at this university, as he saw it, with that in his home country. With considerable bitterness, he said:

> This is a terrible university! 'Grotesque,' I would call it. I did learn a lot in my field, but you're left too much on your own here. Everything is very individual — no relations with anyone. I did some graduate work back home before coming here and it was very different. I was treated very well there. Faculty there related to you and worried about you. Here, it's a different system — faculty are too busy publishing to pay attention to you.

Clearly, students' evaluations of the predissertation years rest as much, if not more, on the extent to which they perceive faculty interest, helpfulness, and supportiveness, than on a more objective assessment of the academic quality of their courses. And it appears that the more prestigious the department, as indicated in the 1982 (Jones et al.) ratings, the less do students see their professors as individuals with whom they can establish satisfactory relationships and upon whom they can call for advice and help.

This finding was reversed, however, in the case of the two engineering departments studied. Here, students were uniformly pleased with their early experiences in the more prestigious department and dissatisfied with their course years in the less prestigious one. In the former department, students rated some courses as excellent while others were rated less than good. They also saw some faculty as "really fine" while others were, as one put it, "pitiful." Some students felt that there were too few electives; others noted that several advanced courses were "not that advanced". But overall, there were few complaints either about poor course quality or about faculty neglect. In fact, there were almost no complaints at all, with the exception of two students — one Chinese the other a Pakistani — who thought that more attention should be given to the way in which teaching assistants were selected. Said the Pakistani:

> Look, I'm a TA, but I should definitely have been screened more

carefully. I wasn't prepared to teach. My English was very poor, and I don't think I knew the subject well enough.

The student from China agreed:

To make up for a shortage of faculty, they get graduate students to teach — and that's not good.

The department chairman acknowledged this as a problem but explained that there is now little choice but to give teaching assistantships to some foreign students whose English might be less than adequate. This is because the overwhelming majority of the graduate student body is foreign, with Orientals whose language deficiency was most acute, making up the largest segment of the foreign student population.

Interestingly, at this university foreign students were considerably less likely than those at other schools to report problems of adjustment due to difficulty with the English language. One reason, of course, is that the nature of the subject (engineering) involves more emphasis on the universal language of mathematics and less on English per se. But in addition, in an environment where foreign students predominate and many have similar language difficulties, each individual student may feel less handicapped.

In the less prestigious engineering department, there was unanimous criticism both about the quality of the courses and instruction and about faculty neglect. All the students interviewed felt that there were insufficient faculty to teach all of the various courses that should be taught and that, as a result, a number of the graduate courses listed in the catalogue never got taught. An American student explained:

Faculty have much too great an undergraduate load and that means only limited time for graduate courses. So some of the graduate courses just don't get taught.

A Lebanese student complained that there were big gaps,

that is, areas that were not covered by courses. He also noted that the prerequisites for courses were not clear:

> There's a lot that should be reformed in this department. It's very unclear about what you need in order to take other courses and there's no real advising about this. If you're having problems, especially language problems, as I was, you're in trouble. When I came here I was totally lost. I had one day to set up a program and no one helped me. I had to do it alone. The advisor that they assigned me just signed it blindly, never discussed it with me. Then I found out that I didn't have the background for some of these courses and I did very badly in them.

A critical problem, raised by several students, was that the faculty in the department was not strong enough to attract the kind of research monies that make a department an exciting place for students. Further, lack of sponsored research means lack of research assistantships and this in turn, not only puts financial pressure on students, but also deprives them of faculty contact and of a source of dissertation topics. And finally, at least at this university, the relative paucity of sponsored research sends faculty outside the university — to industry — to supplement teaching incomes with lucrative consulting fees. An American student explained:

> This department needs a lot of improvement. The faculty have very little commitment to research. They're either bogged down with large classes and too much administrative paperwork, or they're busy with their own consulting. Sometimes they're so busy that they just cancel their classes or, worse, send in a TA. The courses, frankly, aren't that bad, but as for research, that's different. There's no direction, no way for us to learn what goes into a good piece of research, no protocol for how to develop a research topic. So when it comes time for the thesis, we have to start from scratch, and we're very much on our own.

Interestingly, the very factors which make for a high departmental quality rating — faculty research and publication —seem to affect students in opposite ways when we compare engineering with the humanities and social sciences. The more prestigious engineering department had no problem securing research monies and, as a result, students — while occasionally complaining about the quality of some courses — had little sense that they were neglected by faculty. Most were engaged as research assistants and were working closely with one professor or a group of professors on projects from which they knew they would eventually derive a thesis topic. In contrast, in the less prestigious engineering department, research monies were limited, research assistantships were less available, and faculty were perceived as too occupied with lucrative consulting to devote time to their classes and students.

In history and economics the reverse was the case. At the less prestigious university, faculty — apparently in an effort to attract better students — were ready to devote more time and attention to teaching and advising. In the more prestigious history and economics departments, according to students, senior faculty were busy with their own research and writing and were uninterested in students; junior faculty were unable or unwilling to stay for long at the university; and, as a result, students were provided with minimum guidance and support. As will be seen in later chapters, these differences between the more and the less prestigious departments are not restricted to the predissertation period; they persist throughout the graduate years and color the relationship of the student with his or her thesis advisor.

The problems engendered by what students perceive as faculty neglect during the predissertation years appear to have particular impact on the foreign student. In fact, it was generally the foreign rather than the American student who complained bitterly about poor advising and lack of faculty support and encouragement. Americans were more matter-of-fact in their criticism and seemed to be less emotionally thrown by departmental or faculty shortcomings. Foreign students, by contrast, spoke with deep feeling about the problems they had experienced during the years when they were fulfilling their course requirements, particularly those problems associated with faculty neglect. And it should be noted, the reverse was the case as well: they expressed considerable appreciation for faculty who they felt had been supportive and encouraging. Such support carried the foreign students through the sharp transition from academia in their home countries, where a student's life was in various ways very different. Thus, an Israeli student missed the informal relationship she had enjoyed with professors back home. An Asian student could not understand the freedom and informality with which Americans address their professors. A Lebanese student found the pressure of quizzes and examinations and the emphasis on grades overwhelming. A Chilean student articulately summed up what he called the "cultural shock" he experienced on coming to a large, prestigious U.S. university:

> Graduate students are treated very well in our country. In a way, we're the privileged, the elite. We all had fellowships. We'd eat lunch every day with our young professors. Then you come here and you're not treated specially at all. Professors here don't think you're special, but our professors in Chile thought that we were. So I came here with a distorted picture of what being a graduate student was. Here, I felt lonely — I didn't know what to do.

Thus, it is no wonder that many foreign students, cast adrift in an unfamiliar environment, look to faculty as more than imparters of information, but rather, as a Lebanese student put it:

> I'd like them to share feelings, problems. I'd like them to be warm and relating, not just all "professor".

In sum, the predissertation years may be particularly difficult for the foreign graduate student especially in those departments where —for whatever complex of factors — faculty are not responsive to students' needs for assistance, encouragement, warmth and support. In the next chapter, we move from the predissertation years to a crucial step for the graduate student along the route to the doctorate, namely, the selection of the thesis advisor.

4
The Choice of an Advisor

"Few decisions in graduate school can have a more profound effect on a student's life or career than the choice of an advisor," says Susan Rasky in a 1985 *New York Times* article about the difficult path to the Ph.D. In principle, prominent advisors can introduce their students into the "proper" academic circles, provide opportunities for pre- and postdoctoral publications, and smooth the way for entry into a position at a prestigious university or a lucrative career in the private sector.

In fact, research confirms that academic sponsorship plays a vital role in students' careers, as measured by their scientific productivity and position during the first postdoctoral decade. A study of a probability sample of doctoral chemists indicates that their sponsors' productivity was positively associated with their own predoctoral productivity and that their sponsors' professional eminence (as measured by the number of honorary degrees received and the number of science advisory committees served on) was consequential for the postdoctoral career of the sponsored student (Reskin 1979).

We turn first, accordingly, to the process by which faculty member and student enter into the advisor/advisee relationship.

Who selects whom? To what extent is the match determined by such factors as the reputation of the faculty person, the availability of research monies, the discovery of mutual interests as a result of a course taken? Is there indeed an element of choice or are assignments perhaps made by the department? Would a particular student have preferred to work with a different faculty member but for one or another reason was unable to do so?

The route to an advisor varies from school to school, from discipline to discipline, and even from student to student. However, there are certain key factors which are almost universal. First, with rare exceptions, faculty and students agreed that the initiative is and, in fact, must be taken by the student. What this means was explained by an engineering professor:

> It's a free market here as far as selecting an advisor is concerned. What I mean is that the student has to sell himself and believe me, there are some who get bounced around. However, I should add that once a student has passed the qualifyings, we feel a commitment to see that he gets an advisor, although we can't force someone to take him on. From the department's point of view, it depends to a large extent upon which professors have (research) money and can therefore support students on their grants.

A member of the same department qualified his colleague's remarks, noting that occasionally a faculty member will take the initiative, precisely because of the need for students to work on funded research.

> We used to wait for them to come to us, but then we found we had the funds and the work so we went searching for good students. What you usually do is wait to see if a student does well on the qualifying exams, or else you hear about a really good student so you go after him. Sometimes you're too late and someone else gets the student!

Students in this department were well aware that the availability of research monies meant that they might be sought out to serve as research assistants and that this would generally result in a dissertation topic with one of the professors in charge of the project serving as thesis advisor:

> I took a course with him and did very well. In fact, I "aced" the exam. So I wasn't surprised when he asked me to come on board as an RA. I guess that means that he's my advisor, although a number of faculty members are working on the project.

Even in engineering, however, where research monies play an important role in bringing advisor and advisee together, most faculty and students agreed that students had to take the initiative. Said one professor:

> If a student has his own ideas, he'll go to that professor whose interests most closely mesh with his. They come to me and I decide whether or not I want to take them on. On what basis? If I'm interested in their ideas, and if I think they have a good chance of finishing. I watch them over a period of time, especially in independent study courses before I'll consider them. After all, I have to trust the people I'm going to work with — their technical ability, their attention to detail, their care with the equipment. I'm very picky and try to keep the numbers small— even two at any given time is too much.

What prompts a student to ask a particular faculty person to serve as thesis advisor? Two factors — either singly or in tandem —generally served as catalysts: a course or courses taken with the faculty person and/or a meshing of intellectual interests.

Most students had taken at least one course with the person who later became their advisor. Sometimes this was because they had entered graduate school with an interest in that person's particular area of specialization. For other students, the subject matter of the course usually combined with an appreciation for the style of the professor, led to a decision to write a thesis in the area and to ask that person to serve as advisor. An engineering student from Syria, for example, said:

> I took his course and decided that the field was one in which I'd like to work. But more importantly, I felt that he would be the best person to work with. Why? As an individual, he's extremely intelligent and what I liked most about him in class is that he lets you think for yourself — he doesn't try to impose what he thinks on you. That's very important in an advisor — I like to be treated as an adult; I don't want a baby-sitter.

A history student (American) echoed these sentiments:

> I got to know him quite well through courses, especially through the seminar, and I really liked him. I felt that he gave us opportunities for lots of freedom of expression and that's important if you are to develop as a professional. He's been the same way as an advisor — he'll give you general guidelines, but he won't do your thinking for you.

Thus, one course, or several courses, not only served to spark a student's interest in a particular area, but also initiated the process of alerting the student to those qualities of a professor which might make him a good advisor.

In few instances, as was seen in the previous chapter, a student had chosen to do graduate work at a particular university — in a particular department — specifically to study under the professor who eventually became the thesis advisor. Said one such history student:

> She's an authority in the field of US/China relations and I chose to come here because of her. In fact, before I transferred here I spoke with her and only made the move after she agreed to serve as my advisor.

An engineering student who had been working at Bell Labs at the time that he decided to go back to school for a graduate degree, said:

I knew the field that I wanted and I knew him (his advisor) by reputation. He does a lot of consulting work for Bell. So when I came here I spoke with him and he agreed to be my advisor.

Several students noted that they literally had had no choice when the time came to seek an advisor. This was generally the case when a student's proposed dissertation was in an area in which only one professor had an interest or expertise. Said an American student who was writing a thesis in twentieth century Polish history:

He was really the only tenured professor in my field; luckily I had no problem getting to him.

And a Lebanese engineering student:

He's the only one in the field. I had no choice.

While mutuality of intellectual interests was generally the major factor leading a student to ask a particular professor to serve as the thesis advisor, other considerations occasionally came into play. Two Latin-American students, for example, noted that they had specifically approached a professor who came from their own background:

When it came to choosing an advisor, I felt it would be a good idea to work with someone from a Latin background — I felt I'd be able to communicate better with him. Also, he was a link with my country — my professors in Chile knew him, and they told me to go and see him when I got to the university. So I used to go to his office and talk with him on an informal basis and then it became natural to ask him to be my official advisor.

An Argentinian student was an advisee of the same professor:

There are several professors here who are working in my area, but he's also from Argentina, and I knew him slightly from the institute from which I got my M.A. He used to lecture there and I felt I'd be able to get along well with him.

But a second Argentinian student chose not to work with that professor, specifically *because* he was from her home country:

> I could have worked with him but he's Latin-American and I didn't want that. Why? For political reasons —I didn't like either his economic orientation or his temperament. My advisor is a real Renaissance type, very widely read, and I like that.

Political considerations also entered into a history student's choice of advisor:

> My dissertation is about the heroes of the Russian emigre movement, that is, the losing side of the Revolution. I felt that [the chosen advisor] would be more convinced than the other possible person in the field that it was worthwhile to study the anti-Marxists. The other professor is a fine scholar, but he's too pro-Marxist for me.

Given that in more instances than not, the initiative of the student is required for the establishment of the advisor/advisee dyad, to what extent may foreign students in general, or foreign students from a particular country, find the process more difficult, or the reverse, than American students? When I asked this question of both students and faculty, few felt that the student's cultural background entered into the equation. That is, neither students nor professors thought that foreign students were either discriminated against or that they were given preferential treatment when it came to acquiring a thesis advisor. Yet most were ready to agree that there were indeed cultural differences between American and foreign students, differences that might well come into play when it came to obtaining an advisor. For example, a number of both faculty and students said that on the whole, American students were more aggressive than foreign students. Several of those interviewed, however, distinguished among different national groups and there was a general consensus among these groups that Israelis and Latin-Americans tend to be more aggressive than students from Korea or China. Said one professor, for example:

> Asian students in particular simply do not want to even suggest that they have a will. They're just not as assertive as they should be — they're afraid that they'll offend. It's an extreme form of politeness which is pleasant, but not functional for doing research where the idea is to challenge.

Another differentiated between the Chinese, who he felt were quite aggressive —"they come and demand"— and the Koreans who were just the opposite.

> The Koreans are not at all aggressive. I'm a father image to them. Even after several years, they're still bowing to me.

Extreme politeness and lack of aggression not only may be dysfunctional for doing the kind of independent research required for the doctorate, but also may place the student with these characteristics at a disadvantage when it comes to exercising the initiative needed to obtain a thesis advisor. Said one professor:

> Typically, students have to take the initiative if they want us to serve as thesis advisor. The Koreans are doubly disadvantaged. They're much more timid about approaching us — American students and Israelis are much more pushy. And they have a terrible language problem which limits their general participation in the department. This can be a real disadvantage in getting an advisor —they're just not visible.

The above suggests that the problems which some foreign students may encounter at the stage of selecting an advisor begin far earlier in the student's graduate career. At all four universities, professors and students, department chairmen and directors of International Student Offices, agreed unanimously that foreign students in general, but Asian students in particular, enter the university with severe language handicaps. Said an engineering professor:

> Theoretically they have to take remedial courses if their proficiency in English is not up to at least a minimal level. But somehow, it's not enough. There's a tremendous language problem with at least half of the foreign students and with almost all the Asian ones. I can't tell you what a barrier it is, even in our field which is so quantitative. I feel very strongly that they should require more English proficiency —it's a serious impediment to exchange of information.

From the time they enter the university, this impediment affects the academic and social life of foreign students. Several Asian and Middle Eastern (Arab) students said, for example, that it had taken them several years to develop the confidence to speak up in class. Others noted that compared with American students, they had had to spend double and triple the time reading assignments and writing papers. Some said that language barriers had inhibited their developing "after-class" relationships with professors. Lack of facility in English, however, was not the only factor inhibiting the development of informal relationships with faculty. As a Malaysian student explained:

> We have a different sense of the student professor relationship. We see [professors] too much as authority figures. At home there's much more of a gap between us. Americans are more open, aggressive, and informal with professors, so they get to know them better during the time we're taking courses. Then it's not so hard to go to them and ask them to be your advisor.

The foreign student is handicapped in yet another way when it comes to the process of obtaining an advisor. Just about every American graduate student interviewed, but fewer than one in four of the Asian students, had held positions as teaching assistants (TA's) in their departments. As one department head explained:

> American students have a tremendous advantage getting the TA

jobs. First of all, of course, is the language problem — particularly for students from China or Korea or some of the Arab countries. But even if they don't have a language problem, foreign students often do have a problem as TA's because they have difficulty relating to American undergraduates.

He went on to say:

American undergraduates can be very aggressive and an American TA understands this and knows how to deal with them. But it infuriates and frustrates the foreign student; he can't handle it. Foreign students see undergraduates as overly demanding, as one big burden and they refuse to make themselves accessible to them. And the undergraduates rightfully complain about it. So it's very rare that I give foreign students TA appointments.

Mahdi et al. (1986) agree that foreign teaching assistants face not only the general problems of any beginning teachers, but also those of teaching classes in a language in which they are not fully proficient and in an academic environment that is unfamiliar. They suggest that foreign teaching assistants may confront problems arising from cultural differences such as concepts, words, symbols, and gestures that may have "culturally significant meanings that may vary from country to country."(p.10)

A Lebanese student mentioned another factor that may make it impossible for some foreign students to become teaching assistants:

Even if my English was (sic) adequate, which you can see is not the case, I could not have become a TA. I am on a scholarship from my country and I am not permitted to work. It is a big disadvantage because it isolates me. I have no professor that I can deal with on a regular basis. Being a TA is a big advantage.

Inability to serve as a teaching assistant has a number of disadvantages, then, over and above the obvious financial one. In more instances than not, the professor for whom the student was serving as a teaching assistant later became the official thesis advisor. As an American student said:

> I would meet him on an almost daily basis and very often we would talk about things not necessarily related to the course. He was a good person to use as a sounding board for testing out my half-baked ideas for the thesis. It just became natural for him to be my thesis advisor.

An Israeli student (who spoke English well) echoed the above:

> I had no trouble at all getting him to sign on as my advisor. After all, I had TA'd for him and we had gotten to know each other quite well.

Even when the TA/professor relationship did not always evolve directly into the student/sponsor one, according to some students it facilitated their acquiring a thesis advisor. Often, the professor for whom the student was serving as TA acted as a preliminary, informal advisor and later recommended the student work with a particular colleague, in some instances putting in a good word for the student with that colleague.

Over and above the issue of access to an advisor, the TA experience serves as a valuable form of professional socialization. After all, as a TA the student has the opportunity to interact with a professor on a regular, and often informal, basis. In the process, the student becomes more than just one in a sea of often anonymous faces in the classroom and, as the two meet frequently outside of the classroom, the relationship begins to change from the strict student/professor one to that of two colleagues. The old barriers begin to crumble, as often evidenced by a first-name relationship, and the professor is seen in a less awesome or authoritative light.

Nor should the possible future professional rewards of serving as a TA be minimized. For it provides first-hand experience behind the desk of a classroom, as well as knowledgeability about the many other facets of teaching: preparing and grading exams, evaluating term papers, or setting up syllabi. Serving such an apprenticeship is likely to give the student an edge in the competition for a post-graduate academic position.

A second type of apprenticeship is somewhat more available to foreign students, namely, the research assistantship. A number of foreign engineering students were serving as research assistants on projects from which they had been able to derive a thesis topic. Research assistantships also facilitate the acquisition of an advisor as one of the professors directing the overall project on which the student is working often comes to serve as the student's official thesis advisor. Few research assistantships, however, were to be had in either the history or the economics departments studied. In those departments, it was the teaching assistantship which both provided valuable professional socialization, and facilitated the process of acquiring a dissertation advisor.

It would appear, then, that a combination of factors give the American student an edge over the foreign one when it comes to the critical matter of obtaining a thesis advisor. Language handicaps make foreign students reluctant to speak up in classes or after classes, thus making them less visible to professors. At the same time, culture traits peculiar to some home countries —extreme deference or lack of aggressiveness — make it difficult for certain foreign students to exercise the kind of initiative that may be required to obtain a thesis advisor. And finally, language problems, culture traits, or home country restrictions on employment may operate to create a major structural barrier for foreign students in that they may find it difficult or impossible to obtain the TA'ships which help nourish professional socialization in general and which often facilitate the acquisition of a thesis advisor.

5
A Researchable
Topic

Perhaps one of the most difficult aspects of writing a doctoral dissertation is that of narrowing down a broad interest into a researchable topic. Some graduate students, by the time they have completed their coursework and taken their field exams or comprehensives, have a general idea of the substantive area in which they would like to work. It is at this point that they will approach that faculty person (or those faculty persons) whose area of interest coincides with their own. Other students, in contrast, have not carved out a specific area of interest, much less a researchable topic. As one professor, in history, explained:

> There are no general rules. It depends on the student and his or her background. But I'd say there are two types: those who come in knowing perfectly well what they want to do and also knowing just who we are and what they can get from us. Others come because they like "history" in the broad sense. They have no specific ideas and it takes a long time to focus them. Frankly, I like the ones who know what they want.

Between these two extremes are the students described above — those who may have at least a general idea for a thesis topic but require considerable assistance in narrowing down this interest into a manageable research question. Almost every professor noted that he tended to play a major role in this process, even though he would have preferred that the student take the initiative in this respect. Said one engineering professor:

> I try to get them to take an active role in the zeroing in process. I want them to play to their own strengths, that is, to carve out a thesis that relies on math if that's what they are strong in, or on theory if they have that kind of ability. Unfortunately, most of them get caught up in topics that I mention to them. The problem is that this can delay them because then they have to develop a background in that area.

He went on to say that foreign students, in particular, had a problem with the dissertation topic:

> They keep asking what I want them to do — particularly the Asians. It's very hard to get them to take the initiative because they're afraid that they'll offend me. It's an extreme form of politeness which is pleasant, but not functional for doing independent research.

Said another engineering professor:

> Sometimes I have a specific, well-defined topic that I'm interested in and I transfer it to the student — but that's not how I like to do it. I like to take a much broader, less directive approach. That is, the student begins to generate ideas; you have a few "give-and-take" sessions; you direct the student to the literature and then try to get the student to pick a sub-area. But, unfortunately, it doesn't usually work this way. You need a student who's quick to learn, self-motivated, technically good, and a real self-starter — and most students are not.

In engineering, particularly at the more selective university, the choice of a research topic appeared to hinge largely on the kinds of research projects which were being carried out under government and industry contracts. A professor who, with several colleagues,

46

was engaged in a good deal of such contractual research, explained:

> Things have changed here. It used to be that I would encourage students to explore and gradually arrive at a workable topic. They generally had ideas, especially those who had worked at a place like Bell Labs. Lately, however, we're generating so much work because of contracts, that our RA's tend to select their topics from the research that we're doing in the group. I used to try to be less directive; now I really insist that they select a decent research problem within our context so that they are somewhat less free to explore.

Some students are less than happy with these restrictions. Said an Asian student:

> The trouble is that in this department the research world is too much influenced by the world of industry. It's all a question of where the money is — what the government or the big companies are willing to pay for. That narrows our choices as far as a topic for our dissertation is concerned.

Another student recognized these constraints but accepted them without resentment. In fact, he felt that a certain element of choice still remained:

> I see it as an interactive process. True, he (the advisor) did tell me his research problems — in fact he prioritized them. But he also said that I could work on any problem that I dream up *as long as it meshes with the group's work*. It just so happened that the problems he outlined were interesting to me, so I was happy to take his suggestions. I guess I could have done something else, but I recognized the boundaries and made sure that I fitted in.

Yet another student in that group, while recognizing the constraints, felt he was fortunate in having his topic carved out for him:

> You get to realize how important it is to work on a topic that is part

of your advisor's work. One student I know, for example, was very upset because he wasn't getting enough time and help from his advisor. He realized that it was because he was working on his own topic, something not related to his advisor's work. I'll tell you — it's much better to be working on something close to your advisor's work. You'll get more time because there's more at stake for the professor.

This particular student, a Pakistani, thought there were advantages in being able to carve out a thesis topic from the contract research projects:

Actually it's good — we're working on contracts, but it's mostly research we would want to be doing anyway. This way, we get more direction, but not necessarily pressures. That is, we can still use our own initiative, but at the same time we don't feel the pressure to come up with our own ideas.

In the engineering department at the second university, research monies were considerably less abundant and most graduate students were working individually with a professor rather than in a group involved in a contract. Some students felt that this worked to their disadvantage. An American student said, for example:

The problem here is that there is not enough sponsored research in this department, so you have to define your objectives by yourself. Other schools give you a topic, you know, "here's something that is being sponsored." RCA or Bell will define the relevant topics that are current. But we have very little of that here. I had to find a topic on my own on an unsponsored project.

When I asked him what role his advisor had played in the definition of the topic, he grimaced and said:

He gave me a very broad topic and sent me off on my own to investigate it and narrow it down. I literally spent two and one-half years spinning my wheels because I wasn't given adequate direction in developing the topic.

This student's advisor was the one quoted above who had said that he preferred not to transfer a specific, well-defined topic to a student, but rather to send the student to research the literature on a very broad topic and to get the student to pick a sub-area for the dissertation. Apparently, this is not what his advisees prefer, for a second advisee of this same professor also complained about the lack of direction in narrowing down a topic. Said that student (from Lebanon):

> I guess you could say that he put me on the highway, but I must say that I got very lost and I feel that it's taking much too long as a result.

Unfortunately, this advisor and his two advisees have very different expectations regarding the role of the sponsor in helping the student focus on a thesis topic. The students feel that the advisor should be more directive, rather than letting them flounder for several years in search of a researchable topic. The advisor, on the other hand, feels that:

> It's important that the student develop a broad picture of the field and gradually, through an interactive process with me, begin to narrow down his focus. I like to see the student make the major contribution to this process.

In the field of engineering, topics for dissertations tend to emerge from the research grants and contracts on which faculty and students (as research assistants) are working as a team; but in economics and history, the process is somewhat different. Several professors suggested that broad ideas for a dissertation tended to develop in the course of a seminar or colloquium the student has taken with them. Then the process of narrowing down commenced with some advisors playing a more and others a less active role. The preference of almost all, however, is for the latter. Said a history professor:

I feel that it's mainly their problem, although I'll help if they ask. I guess I'm a "libertarian" —that is, I'm less directive than most of my colleagues. If a student is having a hard time, I'll try to help. For example, I may warn them against a topic that I think they won't be able to handle. Frankly, I think most students would prefer that I take a more directive role than I do.

While one of his advisees was quite satisfied with this "libertarian" approach, ("I knew exactly what I wanted to do and he liked the idea, so there was no problem.") another was clearly irked by the lack of direction:

I had to do it all myself; there was really no direction. I got almost no input or feedback from him.

Another history professor was somewhat more directive:

I encourage them to come with suggestions which have usually emerged as a result of a course or a seminar that they took with me. Then we discuss it further. I'd say that I tend to play an active role, but I never actually assign or give them a topic. It's a very slow process of discuss, refine, change, rediscuss.

A third history professor was quite willing to help a student focus on a topic but insisted that the topic itself had to be one that the student had developed:

My first task is to help them narrow the topic down. I do this with persistent questions, trying to force them to play an active role and making sure that they are really interested in the subject. Frankly, if I have to give a student a topic, I do my best to try to discourage that student from continuing. The ones I really like are those who come in with an idea and can run with it, sometimes in an unexpected direction. In cases like that, the process can be very exciting and intellectually challenging for both of us — a real mutual exchange of ideas.

I asked her whether she was more likely to have this kind of mutually satisfying relationship with American or with foreign students.

> It's not a question of whether they are foreign or American, but rather whether they came here for the right or the wrong reasons. That is, are they really serious about getting a degree and genuinely interested in an area? Or are they hanging around waiting to grow up? Or have they been sent by their country but are not really prepared to do serious analytical thinking? The latter, unfortunately is too often the case for the Chinese student.

Since the ability to think analytically seems essential for the entire process of completing a doctoral dissertation, I asked her to expand on her statement that the ability to analyze is often lacking in the Asian student. She explained:

> The American student can understand the analytical process more easily than the Asian student. Asians are good at massive research and at laying it out in a way that's well organized and neatly labeled — very orderly and credible. It's not really a lower standard, but I guess you could call it a reasonably different standard. In China, the main emphasis throughout their education is for the clearest naming and labeling and that's what serves as analysis. As research, it's beautiful; as analysis, it's limited.

An Asian student stated the same idea somewhat differently. He said:

> The courses we took in China were more in depth, less broad. As a result, we're not used to having to exercise our own initiative to get to the bottom of something. The Chinese tend to be 'knowledge-absorption' oriented, while Americans are more 'problem-solving' oriented.

Perceptions about the actual role that the advisor plays in helping the student focus on a researchable topic are not always mutual. An economics professor, for example, said that once a student approached him with a broad idea, he tended to take on an active and directive role:

Usually, they come in with an idea. We talk about it and in the process, I think of relevant material and I direct them to the literature. Then they come back, we talk again and begin to narrow down the focus. I ask them to write a few pages, and then we go on from there. I really keep on top of them; otherwise they can waste a whole year at this stage. I won't let them go off exploring a topic that I think has little promise. I used to be more "liberal" but I found it counterproductive. Students need a more directive approach.

His students didn't see it that way at all. Said one with acerbity:

He was no help at all. In fact, I showed him one idea I had and — I know you won't believe this — six months later I found that he had just written a paper based on that idea. I'm not saying that he actually took my idea and ran with it, but he could have at least told me that he was working in that area and then sent me off in another direction.

Few students have more than just an amorphous idea which they think might be suitable for a dissertation topic and they rely on the advisor to play an active role in helping them to zero in on a researchable topic. Sometimes, a student with an idea has to "shop around" until he either finds a professor who agrees to take him on as an advisee or until he comes up with a topic that interests a professor. A young man from Portugal told of his odyssey:

I approached one professor with a topic and got the feeling that he was bored to the bottom of his mind. I got no feedback at all from him, not a bit of encouragement. I decided that I had better switch subjects or else I'd be totally finished. I lost a whole year doing this. Then I tried another professor with a new topic and, again, I got nowhere. Finally, I went to (current advisor) with an idea that I felt certain would interest him and then I got some feedback. He was nice and really helped me develop the topic.

Other students come with a clear notion of what they want to do, in some cases an extension of a Master's Thesis, in others a topic emerging from the research the student was doing as a research assistant. Is there any difference between American and foreign students as far as the problem of zeroing in on a thesis topic is concerned? For the most part the answer is no, but with some qualification. For example, the students who seemed to have the most difficult time tended to be those with language problems, particularly those from the Far East. An Asian student in history spoke of the difficulties he had:

> I had a very difficult time choosing a topic. I told her my idea and she wasn't at all happy with it. She said it was not manageable and she really discouraged me. But then she pointed out several other possibilities and I just picked one of them. At first I was upset, but now I realize my first idea was a poor one and much too broad. What I'm doing now is much narrower and more exciting —but I never would have thought of it on my own.

An Iranian student said that he had originally settled on a very different topic from the one on which he was now working, as well as on a different advisor.

> I wasted a lot of time, however, because that advisor never suggested that the topic was beyond my ability to handle. Why was it beyond my ability? Because of my very poor English. It was much too theoretical and my language problems made it impossible to understand the literature adequately. Then I settled on a different topic, one that was much more mathematical —just six or seven key independent variables. After all, math is an international language. My only problem then was whether I could get to the data I needed. He (present advisor) was wonderful about checking to make sure I could get the data and then he introduced me to the key people where the data were.

Although there was considerable variation, in general the American student was more likely to have a fairly well-formed idea of what s/he wanted to do, while the foreign student — in particular those from Far Eastern or Arab countries — needed considerably more direction in the difficult process of narrowing down a topic. It appears that the same lack of the initiative required to convince a professor to serve as the thesis advisor can cause difficulties for the student as s/he tries to narrow down the thesis topic. Most advisors favor those students who come in with clear ideas for a dissertation topic, and therefore the majority of professors are reluctant to guide foreign students in the process of reducing a topic to manageable proportions.

Students who serve as research assistants have an advantage in that they are often able to carve out a thesis topic from the research they have been working on with a professor who is, in all likelihood, the advisor. These fortunate ones are more likely to be foreign students, only because foreign students currently constitute the majority of doctoral candidates in engineering, where such research assistantships are found. Students who have already written a Master's Thesis — and these are more likely to be Americans — have a decided advantage in that the doctoral dissertation generally represents an extension of an idea on which they have already written.

Foreign students in the humanities and social sciences, however, seem to encounter more difficulties than their American counterparts when it comes to the problem of selecting a topic and narrowing it down to manageable proportions. Language handicaps which persist, earlier academic experience which emphasized knowledge-gathering, rather than problem-solving, cultural norms which dampened initiative and created a sense of awe and unapproachability about professors — all of these are likely to create stumbling blocks for foreign students as they seek to embark on the dissertation.

Once a topic has been selected and its parameters mutually agreed upon, the long process of doing the research and writing the thesis really begins. It is during this period, which may extend from one year to many, many years that the advisor/advisee relationship gels and the pattern of interaction solidifies. The next section will examine various patterns which may emerge as the student moves toward completion of the dissertation.

6
Mentors and Supervisors

To this point, we have looked at the odyssey of the graduate student as s/he selects a university at which to pursue graduate study, completes course work and begins to think about a dissertation topic, seeks an advisor or sponsor with whom to work on the thesis, and then engages in the often long and arduous task of narrowing down a broad idea into a manageable and acceptable dissertation topic with varying degrees of input and direction on the part of the thesis advisor. We have seen that at many points along the route the foreign student tends to be handicapped, sometimes because of language difficulties, but more often perhaps, because of cultural factors which make for a more problematic relationship with faculty than that experienced by the American doctoral student.

We turn now to a description and analysis of the student/advisor dyad itself as the student engages in the actual task of research for and writing of the dissertation. What is the nature of the relationship between the two principals? By this point, student and professor are no longer strangers to one another —particularly if the student has served as the advisor's teaching or research assistant. Does the relationship become less formal? More diffuse? Under what conditions does the student see the advisor as a mentor and what form does mentoring take, if it occurs? When do advisors perceive themselves as mentors and, more importantly, are the perceptions of student and advisor mutual? And finally, can patterned differences be discerned in the dyadic relationship when the student is foreign as compared to American?

Viewing the question from the perspective of the student, the data suggest that students saw their advisors as falling into one of three categories: mentors, conscientious supervisors, or nominal supervisors. These are not necessarily pure types in the Weberian sense but each advisor can be characterized as having more ingredients of one than of the other two types.

Mentorship

Daniel Levinson (1978) suggests that "the mentor relationship is one of the most complex, and developmentally important, a man can have in early adulthood." The term mentor is sometimes rather freely used as a synonym for teacher, advisor, or sponsor. However, we are applying the term to a relationship that encompasses all of these — and more.

The functions of the mentor may include serving as a teacher to enhance the student's skills and intellectual development; a sponsor, using his influence to facilitate the student's entry and advancement in the profession; a host and guide, welcoming the initiate into a new occupational and social world and acquainting the student with the values, customs, and resources of this world; and finally an exemplar, or model, for the student to admire and emulate (Levinson, 1978:98). In a word, says Levinson, the true mentor supports and facilitates "the realization of the Dream," that is, he believes in the student, gives the student his blessing, shares the student's aspirations and hopes, helps the student to define himself as a professional.

The novice, or student, for his or her part, generally regards the mentor with a mixture of admiration, respect, appreciation, gratitude, and even love — combined perhaps, says Levinson, with a tinge of resentment, inferiority feelings, envy, and intimidation. Howell Raines, deputy Washington editor of *The New York Times,* reminisced about his own mentor, a college professor:

> He influenced me more than any man I have known other than my own father. He helped shape my choice of careers and the standards of professional performance by which I judge people to this day. In short, he was my mentor.... A young man cannot will a relationship with a mentor. It must emerge from the flow of two lives and it must have the reciprocity of a good romance. The adulation of the younger man must be received with a sheltering affection that, in time, ripens into mature respect between equals. Carried to full term, it is a bond less profound but more complex and subtle than that between father and son, a kinship cemented by choice rather than biology. (Raines; 46)

Levinson's discussion of mentoring is confined to males as both mentors and mentees, as he is concerned with the developmental patterns that can be found at various stages in the lives of men. He assumes that mentors of younger men are themselves male. This research also provides an opportunity to explore mentoring by and toward women.

Aside from Levinson's work, there has been some research to date on the mentor/mentee relationship, but this largely deals with mentors and their protégés in the business rather than in the academic world. What research does exist, however, suggests that behind the mystique of mentoring lies a group of *behaviors*, rather than a set of innate attributes or personality characteristics of individuals (Alleman et al. 1984). That is, there appear to be no personality profiles that differentiate mentors from non-mentors, or protegees from their non-protégé peers. But in these particular dyadic relationships, mentors behave and are expected to behave differently toward their proteges than non-mentor/ supervisors toward their subordinates. For example, Alleman et al. (1984) constructed a Leadership Development Questionnaire comprised of specific behaviors exemplifying mentoring functions and found significant differences between mentors and non-mentors in such behaviors. Specifically, Stein (1981) found that doctoral students expected their mentors not only to help them with their dissertation research, but to include them on their research teams, assist them in finding their first jobs, and educate them in the "rules of the game" of their profession.

At first glance, it would appear that the relationship between the professor-thesis advisor and the student-doctoral candidate would provide fertile soil for the development of a mentoring relationship. The student has typically taken several courses or seminars with the professor; he has perhaps served as a teaching or research assistant; the two have spent hours developing a researchable thesis topic which, at least theoretically, is of direct interest to the sponsor. Further, since this dyadic contact generally extends over a period of at least two or three years, there is sufficient opportunity for the sponsor to develop an appreciation for and interest in the advisee that goes beyond the usual professor/student relationship. The student, in turn, will have had ample time to observe and emulate the style and performance of his sponsor as teacher, researcher, thinker, and writer. One would expect that mutuality of intellectual and professional interests, combined with a long-term association between an experienced senior academician and an aspiring novice, would — more often than not — presage the development of a mentor-mentee relationship between the sponsor and the doctoral advisee.

Potentially, there are many advantages, both to student and professor, when mentorship characterizes the relationship between dissertation sponsor and doctoral candidate. Those for the student are obvious. Ideally, mentorship brings students into direct contact with the way in which a mature scholar works; it enables them to acquire a genuine understanding of the mentor's theoretical framework; and it permits them to make the crucial transition from deference to scholarly authority to independent initiatives, originality, and the status of peers. In turn, for faculty members, advisees are potential intellectual disciples who reflect credit on them, and they may be invaluable assistants as well. Thus the establishment of a successful mentoring relationship between faculty advisor and graduate student should be a great boon to both. By the same token, a poor relationship presumably deprives the mature scholar of a fine protégé and damages the career prospects of the graduate student.

Despite the potential advantages, mentoring relationships between the graduate student and his advisor were found in this study to be the exception rather than the rule. And this was true whether the student involved was foreign or American. I asked professors whether they saw themselves as mentors to their advisees, and I asked students whether they perceived their advisors as mentors. In fact, not a single professor was ready to define himself as a mentor to any of his advisees. So, if mutual perceptions are essential to the relationship, none of the 33 dyads studied could be described as involving mentoring.

Five students did agree that their advisors could be termed mentors although, interestingly, none had specifically thought of applying that label before. The remainder felt that the term "supervisor" best described their advisors. This large group, however, was of two opinions regarding the quality of that supervision. Nineteen said that their advisors were conscientious supervisors, while nine saw their dissertation sponsors as merely nominal supervisors.

This chapter examines first the advisor/advisee relationship in the two engineering departments and then moves, in turn, to the history and economics departments, first at the more selective and then at the less selective university. The primary questions to be addressed are:

— Why do professors in all three disciplines tend to reject the label of mentor, and how do they see themselves vis-à-vis their advisees?

— What qualities do students expect in an advisor, and how do their advisors measure up to these expectations?

— Do American and foreign graduate students have similar

perceptions of or responses to the style of their advisors?

The answers to these questions emerge as both professors and students speak about their experiences in advisor/advisee relationships.

Engineering: An Absence of Mentorship

In both engineering departments studied, professors suggested that one of the major ingredients of mentorship would be to guide the student into academic rather than industrial careers. As one engineering professor said:

> Do I see myself as a mentor? No — I don't think so, because 80 percent of my students are lured onto tho industrial path where the rewards are greater. So I don't provide that much academic and intellectual guidance.

A second advisor, also in engineering, said:

> No — I'm not a mentor. Rather, I would describe myself as a very close supervisor. I see students once every week or two for at least one to two hours each time—sometimes in my office, sometimes at home. But I don't see myself as their role model — most of them are going into industry, rather than academics. I guess I could say that I saw my own thesis advisor as a mentor. He's in the department here and it's probably because of him that I'm here today.

This professor's own advisee came closer than any other engineering student to regarding his advisor as a mentor, but he said:

> No — he's a mentor only in the sense that in most ways he represents a role model and I do go to him if I have problems about things like funding or a particular course I'm teaching. But

essentially, I see a mentor as someone who protects you and who hopes that you'll make him look good as a result of your work. I have a mentor like this in industry.

In fact, not one of the engineering doctoral candidates regarded his advisor as a mentor. An Asian student had never heard the term before but after it was explained to him, he said:

No, I don't think I would call him that. Although I would say that he's more than just an advisor because he's concerned about you as a person, not just about the project that you're working on. Not that I've ever needed or asked him for any specific help outside of my project, but I can see that he cares about students.

About the same advisor an American student said:

No — he's not my mentor. I don't think that anyone here is a mentor; they're too busy consulting for industry. I suppose the closest he comes to being a mentor for me is that I guess I see a few qualities in him that, if they rubbed off on me, I'd be better off. What qualities? Well — not his intellectual style, rather his aggressiveness in getting things done — I tend to tinker and procrastinate.

Another engineering student said that indeed he did have a mentor, but that it was definitely not his advisor:

A mentor? Yes — but not my advisor. My father has been my mentor. He's an electrical engineer as well and he's the one who has given me the most direction in life, who's been most valuable in terms of my career interests and plans. I definitely want to go into teaching, but not from what I see here. The professors here, including my advisor, are busy consulting —making money. They cancel classes, send in TA's, miss appointments. My father taught me that you have to have personal ethics and integrity and not be tempted by money. My advisor is the last person in the world that I'd want to emulate.

A Lebanese student concurred:

> No — there are no mentors here. I'm very disappointed because I would love to find one but I've stopped thinking about it. All I want to do now is get finished and out of here.

In one of the two engineering departments, students interacted with their advisors on a regular daily basis and, in general, enjoyed cordial relationships with them. However, none saw these advisors as mentors. In this department, students are engaged in contract research under the aegis of a group of professors with constraints and deadlines imposed by the nature of the project rather than by mutual intellectual and scientific interests. They work in the computer lab in groups and when a problem arises, they either consult with one another or with any one of the four or five faculty persons overseeing the project. Said one sponsor:

> The research projects that we generate today have gotten very big so it doesn't make sense to separate the students. Technically, we each have several students for whom we serve as official sponsor, but all the students in the lab have access to all of us, as well as to one another. Perhaps they lose a bit of the personal relationship with us but, on the other hand, they can benefit from more of us. True, I feel I'm getting a little too removed from students — very little one-on-one relationship. But there's no time. We probably have taken on too much work —there always seems to be a rush.

Under such conditions, it is highly improbable that academic mentorship will flourish.

Yet another factor limits the development of a mentor relationship between engineering students and their sponsors — namely the fact that, at least at one university, most of the doctoral candidates are part-time, rather than full-time students. Part-time students tend to be working at companies such as IBM, Bell Labs, or A.T. & T and as one professor put it:

When they're full-time at least they're working with me on projects that I'm working on, that I'm interested in, and they are right here in the lab so I see them all the time. When they're part-time, they basically have to work on their own. They come in every so often with problems, and to keep me up-to-date, but they get very little help on a regular basis. When they have problems, they tend to talk to someone at work. With full-time students, we're always available — every day; the part-time ones, I probably see only every couple of months.

Interestingly, at this university few of the full-time students are American. One reason is that many American students find it far more lucrative to work in industry than to live on the meager salary of a teaching or research assistant. Foreign students, in contrast, either are not permitted to work off-campus or find it difficult to obtain such jobs. On the one hand, then, the American student is unlikely, because of limited contact, to develop a mentorship relationship with his advisor. On the other hand, while the foreign student is more likely to be enrolled on a full-time basis and to be working on contract research under the aegis of his sponsor, the fact that he is one of perhaps five to ten students working under a group of professors, makes the formation of a mentor relationship unlikely.

History and Economics: Does Selectivity Make for Faculty Neglect?

As we move from engineering to history and economics, we might expect the picture to be somewhat different. Students are more likely to be enrolled on a full-time basis and less likely to be involved in team research on departmental contracts. Rather, they tend to be working in one-on-one relationships with the thesis advisor — a condition under which mentorship may be expected to develop. Interestingly, however, not a single professor, either in history or in economics, felt that he or she played the role of mentor. An economics professor, for example, said:

I see a mentor as a professor with a very dominant personality as well as a very pronounced ideology (regarding theory or methodology) that he gets his students to adopt. Right now, I'm not interested in turning out clones, so up to now I have not been a mentor to anyone. Perhaps as I get older and develop less patience for alternative ways of thinking, I may become one.

His colleague, at the same (prestigious) university, agreed:

I certainly don't see myself as a mentor. Somehow, I think you have more of that in science, or in a discipline like sociology, where professors and students tend to work more closely together. Here people go off on their own. Frankly, I see a good advisor/advisee relationship as one where you just help somebody launch and go off into his own orbit.

I asked him how he thought students felt about this perception of the "good" advisor/advisee relationship and he admitted:

I know that students gripe a lot and say that they don't get enough time. It seems to be a perennial source of discontent in the department. But I find that my best students need very little time — maybe three to five times during the entire dissertation period! I just give them a spark and they go out and do it. The weaker ones need much more — maybe fifteen, twenty, or even thirty times during the dissertation.

And indeed, advisees of both of these two professors did gripe. All but one were extremely disappointed with the amount and quality of the feedback and help they were receiving. Even the one student who was relatively satisfied — a young man from Portugal — did not see his advisor as a mentor, but rather as a conscientious supervisor:

No — I don't see him as a mentor, although I will say that I have gotten a lot from him. His courses were excellent, so if I ever teach, I'll be able to use my notes from them. Also, I like his lifestyle. What I mean by that is that he's not in the paper race. He seems to enjoy his work, his life. He's not after the Nobel Prize.

He's relaxed without being lazy. And I did get good substantive advice and feedback from him — not too often — maybe two or three times a year. I don't like to go too often — my English isn't as good as it should be and I hesitate to disturb him about little things. Whenever I did go, however, I got what I wanted — he listened, advised, and didn't make me feel he was in a hurry.

Clearly, however, this student was an exception for the other advisees interpreted the laissez-faire philosophy of these advisors as pure and simple neglect. From their point of view, there was no relationship — advisors were merely nominal supervisors. An Argentinian student almost bitterly said:

A mentor? Definitely not! I've basically had to do almost everything by myself because I get so little from him. He's been no help —he just doesn't seem to care. I must say though, that he's no different from the rest of the department — no one here seems to care.

I asked this student how he would describe a good advisor/ advisee relationship and he said:

A good advisor would be available three times a week in his office so that if I had a problem or question I could go in and see him. He would want me to come in every week or two to show him what I've been doing. He would give me feedback, either written or verbal, on what I write. I wouldn't want him to tell me what to do, but rather to stop me if I was going off in the wrong direction and to provide intellectual and moral support. Frankly, I've heard of only one professor in the department who does this — a young one —and he's leaving for a tenured position out west — they wouldn't give it to him here!

In general, at this more prestigious university — whether in history or economics — the majority of advisees are unhappy and, in many cases, resentful about what they see as neglect of students on the part of faculty in general and on the part of thesis advisors in particular. One student said:

I used to see my Senior thesis advisor, at Princeton, at least once a week. We had a great relationship. I remember his attitude toward graduate students — he used to invite them to his house for tea or coffee. He was always very interested in his students. I must say that he warned me about student/advisor relationships here, but I didn't understand what he was talking about at the time. I'm sorry now that I didn't go somewhere else.

The problem, as these graduate students see it, is that professors are just not interested in students, not interested in possible interchange of ideas. The student whose senior thesis advisor had cautioned her about coming to this university said of her current advisor:

It's not that he refuses to make himself accessible. He'll say, for example, "come in and talk whenever you want." But never once did we have a good conversation. You get the feeling that you're being rushed. I always saw myself as an intelligent person, but now I've begun to feel that I'm not interesting to talk to. I feel cowed by him. He's just not willing to invest in students, not willing to give, to "really" help.

When I raised the question of mentorship, she laughed:

You don't get that at all in this department. They don't even see us as disciples, to whom they are trying to convey an attitude, a way of seeing things, an appreciation for economics, an understanding of what they are trying to do. You just don't get any kind of scholarly feeling here — it's just a job for them. I'm afraid that the whole nature of higher learning has changed; it's become more of a business than a scholarly enterprise.

Not only did no student at this university see his or her advisor as a mentor, but the majority of students felt that their advisors were giving them minimal or no help with their dissertations. As evidenced by the description above of a "good" advisor, students are not necessarily looking for mentors or for collegial interchange. They basically want to complete a thesis and they seek intellectual

67

input, guidance, and feedback from their advisor. And for most advisees at this university, such input and feedback were not readily forthcoming. A history student put it this way:

> I certainly could have benefitted from some more painstaking efforts to guide me. But no, he left me entirely to my own initiative. In fact, I really felt like a jerk when I was doing my research overseas — collecting my data. He never prepared me for the bases I should touch, and I spent a lot of fruitless time as a result.

A second student in history had a similar response:

> I'm lucky because I work for him in the office here, so I see him every day. But interaction on the dissertation is absolutely minimal. Maybe we touch base on it every so often, and perhaps a gentle hand prodding me once in a while, but no real input.

Economics students at this university were even more bitter than history students about the lack of guidance and input from advisors. One student, whose thesis defense was imminent, claimed that he had met with his advisor for perhaps a total of six to eight hours over the three years during which he was writing his dissertation. He noted, further, that this was not a unique situation at this particular university.

> It's not only that he's a very busy person. Somehow the system at this university is one where no professors really spend time with students. They don't have any respect for students. After a while I stopped going to him — I got the message that I wasn't going to get any substantial help. When I did go to see him he would say something like "Oh, that's interesting" or "That's fine," but you get the feeling that he's not giving you anything of himself — he's just trying to get you out.

A Chilean student also had nothing positive to say about another professor in the economics department of the same university:

All my encounters with him have been disappointing. In fact, I can't think of a single thing about my dissertation that has been the result of his input or encouragement. I always come out of a meeting with him absolutely depressed and sometimes it takes months to recover. Let me give you an example. Two weeks ago, I went to him and said I was having a particular problem, that there was something I didn't understand and that, as a result, I was stuck. I asked if he could help me. What I expected was that he would discuss it with me, but all he said was "write whatever you have and bring it to me." No ideas, no guidelines, no discussion.

Bitterness about the relationship with the thesis advisor does not necessarily stem from inability to set up appointments, although some students were approaching the defense after having had only minimal contact with their advisor. What students, at least at this particular university, complained about was that even when they met with their advisors they received little or no feedback, minimal encouragement or moral support, and, at best, only limited interaction on either a professional or an informal basis. It is this type of supervisor relationship that I have termed "nominal" and it would appear that, as experienced by history and economics students at the more prestigious of the two universities, this nominal supervisory style was the modal one. Professors, in contrast, saw themselves not as neglectful of their advisees, but rather as purposely non-directive, consciously striving to get students to take the initiative in the dissertation process.

It should be noted that both American and foreign students described their relationship with their advisor as unsatisfactory. What distinguished the American from the foreign student, however, was not so much the objective quality of the relationship, but the subjective response to that quality. American students were rather matter-of-fact about the situation. As one put it:

For a while I felt that I was struggling without his help and I must say I was a little resentful. But I realized that I was going to finish with or without his help so I stopped worrying about it. I had picked an area that was really interesting and I had a good friend —a top student — who was working in a closely - related area so we worked together a lot. I guess you could say that he was really my advisor.

In contrast, foreign students seemed to be considerably more resentful of what they saw as neglect by faculty in general and by the dissertation advisor in particular. A Chilean student said, for example:

You're left much too much on your own here —it's all very indi- vidualistic. Faculty never have time to hear what you say, to listen to your problems, to go beyond a very formal, basic relationship. I did graduate work back home in Chile. There I was writing a paper under a sponsor, and I would see him at least two or three hours a week. We'd go over things, point by point, discussing everything. He would help me reorganize things; he really taught me how to write. Back home in Chile, faculty cared about students. Here no one cares. There's no such thing as an advisor here — they're just graders. I find myself always worried, always anxious, always trying to have some kind of relationship with him. But it's a one-way thing, all in my head — he just doesn't care.

An Argentinian woman was similarly distressed by the lack of feedback and response from her advisor. She felt, moreover, that the problem of faculty neglect was more acute for foreign students than for their American counterparts.

Any time I ask for specific advice about how to go on, he's of no help. He just doesn't seem to care. It's disgusting! He's not the only one — from what I see, advising is pretty bad in the whole department. But I think it's a particular problem for foreign students, because we have time pressures. We usually have a deadline to get back to a job, or to our family. And we have special pressures about having to get enough financial support. Also, we're usually older. American students are younger, not in as much of a rush, and I don't think they come with as high expectations about courses and professors and advisors.

70

History and Economics: One-Sided Mentorship

In the less prestigious history and economics departments, advisees were far more satisfied with the quality of their relationship with their advisors. While none of the advisors — three in economics and two in history — saw themselves as mentors to students, three of the five were so regarded by at least one of their respective advisees. Further, no advisee had anything negative to say about his or her sponsor; all were satisfied with the quality of the relationship, as well as with the nature of the advice, assistance, and guidance they were receiving.

Advisors at this university gave interestingly varied reasons as to why they believed that they were not mentors to their advisees. An economics professor, for example, felt that mentorship was impossible, given the heavy load of advisement:

> A mentor? I? No, not at all. With six or seven doctoral, as well as 17 to 20 M.A. advisees at any one time, how could I possibly be?

When asked why he had so many students to supervise, he said:

> I guess that I have a reputation for being 'soft.' I don't throw them out as many of my colleagues do. But, as a result, I find that I can't give them too much time. Given a chance, they'd be in my office all day long, *especially the foreign students.* Compared to the American students, they write miserably, and I absolutely refuse to serve as their copy editor.

He then went on to note another factor that he felt accounted for the absence of mentorship with his students:

> Maybe over the years I was a kind of mentor for one or two students. But being a mentor implies that you see a student with

tremendous potential and you feel that you really want to carry him along and see him get someplace in the profession. Remember —we're not Ivy League here, so there aren't many students like that.

The doctoral advisees of this professor, however, were apparently quite satisfied with the amount and the quality of time they were receiving from their busy advisor. Said an Iranian student:

> I don't quite know what a mentor is, but if it means that I use him as a role model, then I would say yes. I'm a TA now (for someone else) and I sat in on his undergraduate courses to see how he teaches, so that I could use his methods. He's unusually tough as a teacher, but very popular because he has a great personality. Also, I wish I could write like him. I have trouble with English and I know that I write very badly, but he spends a lot of time going over every line that I write. He sets realistic time limits for me, and then he pushes and encourages me to meet them. And he checks each chapter as I finish. I must say he's had a lot of input into the organization and the substance of my thesis — if I were a thesis advisor, that's exactly how I would like to be.

An American advisee of the same professor said that, while she would not call him her mentor, their relationship was definitely more than a straight advisory one:

> He's a really good advisor and I feel that I'm very fortunate. He reads the materials I give him carefully and takes the time to make suggestions. And he does it in a very reasonable time — a few days. He gives excellent feedback and although sometimes he criticizes, at those times he's constructive and helpful. In addition, philosophically we're very similar in our approach to the field. I've worked with him for three years as an RA and during this time we've developed models and written articles together. I'm sure, too, that he'll help me in terms of jobs when I'm ready.

Why then does she say that she does not see him as a mentor?

Well, I think it's because of my personality, not his. That is, I don't see him as role model, not because he is not a fine professional, but because I am not the type to see anyone as a role model — I do my own thing. And maybe there's one other reason. He hasn't introduced me to colleagues, and that's the kind of thing that mentors do.

A second professor in the department said that the probability of a mentor relationship with students was unlikely for several reasons:

First, I don't think that the quality of my own research is that good, and I have had very few publications, so I don't see myself as being able to be a mentor to anyone else. And second, you can't have a mentor relationship with a student unless you can have good intellectual rapport with that student — and that doesn't happen here often. Students here are second-rate. The good ones don't choose us. And then, third, there's the fact that I can't really help them much with their careers. I don't have many connections, and those few that I do have, I don't want to squander on students who aren't that good.

And, indeed, this professor was not seen as a mentor by his students for some of the very reasons he had noted. As an Indian woman explained:

He was a pretty good advisor, although he was quite busy and didn't have too much time for me. I couldn't just go in at anytime and talk to him — if I had a problem, I had to call for an appointment. But whenever I did see him, I got input. He did encourage me and he was helpful. I'm not sure, however, that he'll be able to help me when it comes to getting a job — and I'm at that point now — because it's a very competitive thing. Letters of recommendation are not enough. You need personal connections and I don't think he has them.

A professor in the field of management said that he could recall only one student with whom he had had a mentor relationship and the factor that he emphasized was that a mentor relationship

73

could develop only when the student was working on a topic of central interest to the advisor:

> Over all the years that I've been advising, I can only say that I had a mentor relationship with one advisee. He was doing his dissertation on a topic that I was involved in at the time and we worked very closely together. I helped him get it published and we became close personal friends. In fact, we still enjoy a close personal and intellectual relationship.

When asked if this particular student was American or foreign, he said:

> Oh — American! Probably a majority of the Ph.D. students here are foreign — mostly from India, Taiwan, and South Korea. But somehow, I find that it's much more difficult to communicate with them than with the American students. Most of them, especially from the Far East, have serious language problems and if you're in a 'soft' [non-mathematical] field like mine, not only does reading their drafts become very tedious, but it gets to be a big chore just to communicate. In addition, the Oriental students tend to be overly dependent; they want to check out each step of the way with you. Even one of my brightest students, from India, is like that. I have no doubt that some of them see me as a mentor, especially as I do tend to be somewhat warm and fatherly, and I do get involved in career advice and help. But it's most unlikely that a real mentorship relationship, that is, on both sides, will develop.

It was interesting to listen to this professor as he recalled his own days as a doctoral student and as he spoke, with great affection, about his mentor:

> Mentorship means developing a sense of excitement about lines of work, and that's just what my mentor did for me. I worked with him on my dissertation — on late-stage capitalism —and he was the person who represented my hold on reality as a graduate student, especially in terms of intellectual interests. I would never have gone into the field had it not been for him. But I don't have

that sort of thing today with my students, except for that one that I mentioned.

Note that not only was the one student with whom this professor had had a mentor relationship an American, but that student's dissertation topic had directly addressed the professor's central interest. A Greek student agreed that it was almost impossible to develop a mentor relationship unless one was working on a topic of strong and immediate interest to the advisor:

> Otherwise, unless you push and chase and demand, you won't get much attention. Maybe that's because being a thesis advisor is a thankless job, unless a student's topic is one which may help to advance a professor's own work, or unless it's a topic that is vitally connected to what he himself is working on. I must say though that even though my topic is somewhat removed from his immediate interests, I find him very accessible and easy to work with. I meet with him every two or three weeks and he's always helpful and encouraging. But the relationship is strictly academic — nothing at all personal. It seems to me that if you're serious about getting finished quickly, then by the time you really get to know each other and might begin, perhaps, to develop a mentor relationship, it's too late.

A history professor, specializing in Latin-American studies, also suggested that mentorship was likely to develop only when structural conditions were such that students were working on topics of immediate interest to the advisor:

> I think that you are likely to find professors serving as mentors in fields where there are more professors (like American History). Then professors can be more selective about whom they accept as advisees. They can accept only students who will agree to work on the topics that they (the professors) want.

Although "simply an advisor" from his perspective, his students unanimously perceived him as their mentor. Said a Scandinavian woman:

Yes — I think I would call him my mentor. He steers me in the right direction; he makes connections for me in the field, and now I'm writing my own article for a book that he's editing. While I was doing my research in Spain, I expected that he'd give me the contacts I needed and he certainly did. In fact, he really was wonderful about that. All through the dissertation stage, he's given me tremendous help and lots of moral support. Now that I'm finishing, I expect that he'll help me get a teaching position. And I do expect to stay in contact with him.

Another of his students, a Cuban woman, agreed:

Mentor? I really hadn't thought about it, but I guess that's what you'd call it. He's a sound, productive, excellent scholar with very high productivity and that attracts me. He's been extremely friendly and excellent to chat with —not just about the thesis. I don't hesitate to call him about a personal problem; in a way I feel like a daughter to him — he's a real fatherly type. What I like about him is that when you do something well, he lets you know, and when you're having problems with a section, he's very constructive, very receptive. I think he respects my work, although he would push me more to go faster if I'd let him. I tend to move at a snail's pace, but I admire the opposite in him; he works quickly and well.

Only one of the thirteen advisors interviewed was a woman, a professor of history at this same university. Interestingly she was the only one to suggest that gender might play a role in mentorship and also used as her model the mentors whom she had in both college and graduate school:

I don't see myself that way at all, although perhaps that's how they see me. [As will be seen shortly, that was the case.] Besides, I don't think students look to women for mentoring; it's something that has always been a male-to-male or male-to-female thing, never the opposite.

When asked why she thought this was so, she said:

I see a mentor relationship as somewhat formal, involving the discipline and everything connected with it, but excluding personal relations. It has to be established with clear boundaries. I think that men have a much clearer sense of boundaries than women and they establish them early on. Women tend to have problems with boundaries — they look for more all-encompassing relationships. That's why I think female graduate students get very confused about their role with a male mentor.

Speaking of her own experiences in college and graduate school, she said:

At college I had a mentor, a man, and our relationship was strictly academic — my senior thesis, choosing a graduate program, and that sort of thing. We did become friends after I graduated, but as a student, it was basically a question of my picking his brain. At graduate school, the head of the department took me on. I would call it even more than mentoring. It was a very significant relationship —I was one of the chosen daughters. He said to me,' You must pick my brain and I'll give you anything in it' — and I did. My relationship with him was close, but only about the academic work, not really intimate.

One of her students, an American woman, did in fact see this professor as a mentor. Her description of the relationship, however, suggests that occasionally the line between advisor and friend blurs and may become dysfunctional for completion of the task at hand, namely, the dissertation:

Yes — I would say that she is my mentor. She's absolutely brilliant. She has a way of picking up on something and cutting through to the essence of what you're saying. It's very reassuring. She's an excellent teacher — I use her as a role model in my own classes. She has a way of remembering what everyone said and then tying it all up in a neat conclusion. She writes beautifully, lectures very well, is an excellent story-teller — she makes the subject fascinating.

How about as a thesis advisor?

> She reads my material quickly and gives very good feedback —
> not so much on the details, but she's great on the large concep-
> tual issues. Once in a while she'll attend to the details and I'm
> stunned because I don't expect it — I count on her for the broader
> questions, you know, 'what are the interesting issues?' and that
> sort of thing. But our relationship goes far beyond the disserta-
> tion. She's introduced me to people in various networks and
> arranged for me to give papers. She helped me with a grant
> proposal and I was able to get money as a result. And I know that
> she'll be helpful when I finish, that is, getting a teaching position.
> In addition, we're friends. I can go in and talk with her whenever
> I want and she's interested in knowing what's going on in all
> aspects of my life. On the one hand, she's maternal and makes
> you feel that she's solidly behind you. On the other hand, we're
> friends — we socialize, we play racquetball, just talk.

Interestingly, this relationship between a young woman and her female advisor probably comes closest to Levinson's descrip-tion of mentorship, described earlier as pertaining only to males. Recall, however, that the mentor in this case did not see herself as such and, in fact, felt that women had a more difficult time than men in delineating the proper boundaries of such a relationship. Perhaps it was this particular student whom she had in mind for the student herself noted that the relationship was not free of problems. She said:

> The only problem as I see it is the possibility of some confusion
> between the role of advisor and the role of friend. I worry about
> this in terms of the thesis. That's why I have another advisor also,
> with a little more distance.

The male advisee of this same history professor, a student from China, regarded her as an excellent advisor but in no way as mentor. His reason, after I explained the term:

> No — I don't think it's a good idea to follow one person. I like to

take the best from different people, so I don't believe in this mentor thing. But she has been a wonderful advisor. I meet with her at least twice a week, because I'm her TA, and we talk about my thesis about every two to three weeks. I write a chapter and give it to her. She makes comments and gives advice. I take most of it and then write a second draft and she comments again. She's very helpful and never makes me feel bad. She encourages me and pushes me to make my arguments stronger. I think she has been a big help in getting me to overcome the typical Chinese submissiveness.

Conclusions

The Advisor's Perspective

The comments of both professors and students make it very clear that mentorship, as described at the outset of this chapter, is not typical of advisor/advisee relationships in any of the six departments studied. Without exception, professors were unwilling to describe themselves as mentors. They were quite aware of the meaning of the term; they understood well that it implied more than merely serving as advisor or thesis sponsor. In fact, when the question of mentorship was raised, several spoke with fond recollection of their own mentors, professors who had instilled in them a love of a discipline and an approach to its study, had launched them on an academic career, introduced them to colleagues, served as a role model, and permitted them to enjoy a relationship that extended beyond the four walls of the campus office.

Professors cited various factors that made mentorship, at least for them, a rare phenomenon. Engineering professors spoke of their inability to steer graduate students into academia rather than into more lucrative careers in industry. Further, certain structural conditions in the engineering departments studied tended to preclude the development of mentoring relationships. Many doctoral students are already working at full-time jobs in industry and, therefore, spend minimal time at the university. While advisor and advisee may meet periodically, there is hardly sufficient time for them to develop more than an instrumental, if cordial, relationship. Further, full-time students are often working in groups on sponsored research projects under the direction of four or five professors from the department. While there may be advantages to this arrangement, in terms of having both other students and several professors at hand for guidance — and the students in the group felt that this was indeed an advantage — mentorship is not as likely to develop as it might in a one-on-one relationship.

Another structural condition is departmental size. Several professors noted that mentoring is unlikely to develop unless there is sufficient leeway in the acceptance of advisees so that professors can accept students who are working on topics of direct and immediate interest to the advisor. They suggested that in larger departments with more professors available to serve as sponsors such selectivity may be more feasible and mentorship more likely to develop. Clearly, however, this is not the case, for even in the larger subspecialties, such as American History or International Trade, professors interviewed did not see themselves as mentors to their advisees.

Professors cited several other factors that they felt precluded mentoring. Younger professors noted that they felt inadequate for the role of mentor. One said, for example, he had not advanced sufficiently in the discipline to be able to serve as a role model, while another commented he had not as yet developed a theoretical or methodological weltanschauung that he might transmit to students. Some noted a heavy load of doctoral and masters advisees made mentoring near impossible. Others, particularly in the less selective departments, suggested the scarcity of students with high academic potential tended to preclude the development of a mentoring relationship with advisees.

How *did* professors characterize their relationship with their doctoral advisees? Essentially they seemed to feel that thesis advising is a necessary but not particularly welcome component of the job. Several specifically noted, in fact, that one receives no "brownie points" for doctoral advising. They saw their role as that of supervisor and their task as that of shepherding their advisees through the dissertation stage in a reasonable amount of time. Some devoted more and others less time and effort to this task. Some were more conscientious than others about reading chapters, editing students' writing, and providing relatively rapid and helpful feedback. On the whole, however, their perception of the ideal advisee was that of a self-motivated, self-directed student who requires only minimal guidance and direction. All recognized that one of their responsibilities is to sponsor the student's entry into the profession and depending upon their evaluation of the student, they complied either with pro forma letters of recommendation or with more energetic efforts to help students obtain employment. Several (in engineering) had collaborated with advisees on papers, but this was not a common occurrence.

In sum, from the perspective of professors, there is little excitement to be derived from serving as dissertation sponsor, little feeling of sharing of mutual interests and concerns, little sense of pride and satisfaction in actively helping the student develop into a colleague and peer. In a word — an absence of mentorship.

The Advisee's Perspective

Students' descriptions and evaluations of the advisor/advisee relationship lead to the conclusion that this relationship represents an extension of general faculty/student relationships in a department. For example, in the less selective engineering department as well as in the more selective history and economics departments, criticism of faculty as teachers at the predissertation stage abounded. Professors were seen as too busy with industrial consulting or publishing to concern themselves with the problems of students, or simply as aloof or uninterested in matters of student advisement. And it was precisely in these three departments that sponsors were seen as nominal supervisors —remote, diffcult to approach, remiss in providing concrete help and feedback. In fact, all nine students who described their advisors as merely nominal were from these three departments and not a single student from any of the three departments saw the advisor as a mentor.

In contrast, students in the other three departments — the more selective engineering and the less selective history and economics departments — were relatively satisfied with their professors during the predissertation years. They described them as interested in the concerns of students, ready to offer advice and guidance, and excellent classroom models. And it was in these three departments that students described their thesis advisors as either conscientious supervisors or as mentors. It would appear then that mentoring or good advising may be less a matter of personality than of structural conditions in a department or a university conducive either to attention to, or neglect of, the concerns of students.

The American vs. the Foreign Advisee

The comments of both professors and students suggest several conclusions about differences between American and foreign doctoral students with respect to the advisor/advisee relationship. First, we should note, however, one area of agreement. With only a few exceptions, American and foreign students of a given advisor tended to render similar judgments about the quality of advising they had received. In no instance, for example, was an advisor seen by an American student as a mentor, but by a foreign student as a nominal supervisor — or vice versa. At most, disagreement could be seen between the categories of mentor vs. conscientious supervisor, or conscientious vs. nominal supervisor. Even in these cases, however, sometimes a foreign student's evaluation and at other times that of an American advisee, was the more favorable one. Further, two of the three professors who were seen as mentors by advisees were so perceived both by their American and their foreign advisees. In the third case, the American student described her advisor as a mentor while the foreign advisee saw that advisor as a top-rate supervisor. Similarly, American and foreign students were generally in agreement about four professors who were described by most of their advisors as merely nominal supervisors.

This consensus suggests that advisors tend to treat all their advisees in relatively similar manner according to their particular style of advising. Thus there is no evidence either that professors discriminate against foreign students as far as giving time and help is concerned or, on the contrary, that thesis advisors devote special attention to their foreign advisees.

What does differentiate American and foreign students, however, is their expectations of their advisors as evident from their definition of mentorship on the one hand and their response to the nominal supervisor on the other. For foreign students, mentorship appears to be limited to the task at hand — the writing of the dissertation. Those who saw their advisors as mentors described them as generous with their time, ready to provide guidance, support, direct help, encouragement. They spoke of advisors who read and edited the material submitted to them in a reasonable amount of time and who provided both substantive and organizational input for the dissertation. Some also noted that they saw their advisor as a role model, both as teacher and as writer.

American students tended to call this kind of advising good, perhaps even excellent, supervising, but not mentoring. For Americans, mentoring involved considerably more. They looked less for substantive assistance and editing but more for a kind of mutual relationship, an opportunity for co-authorship, introductions to colleagues, a strong helping hand when it came to entry into the profession. Without at least some of these ingredients, advisors were seen merely as dissertation supervisors.

Foreign students, in other words, equated mentoring with good supervising. American students, in contrast, saw mentoring in the classic sense of the term, as a relationship that was gradually evolving into a collegial one. The expectations of the two groups are different. Foreign students, particularly those from Asian countries, are likely to hold professors in awe and to see them as strong authority figures. They are accustomed to faculty who maintain a considerable measure of distance between themselves and their students. Coming from a cultural background, therefore, that precludes informality, much less colleagueship, between professor and student, the foreign student is unlikely to expect this type of relationship to develop between himself and his dissertation advisor.

American and foreign students also differed in their response to the nominal supervisor. American students are angry, annoyed and resentful but, at the same time, not devastated by the absence of attention, assistance and input from the advisor. They tend simply to get on with the task of finishing the dissertation, sometimes turning to peers, sometimes to another professor, for support and feedback. They were generally quite acute in diagnosing the cause for the situation: an advisor who was overloaded with administrative responsibilities or industrial consulting, or a general departmental or university-wide ambiance of indifference to students.

Foreign students, in contrast, were devastated and in several cases seemed almost paralyzed, powerless to move ahead, to get on with the task at hand. They spoke bitterly about advisors who did not read their material, who were unavailable for meetings, and who were not willing to provide concrete direction and assistance. But even more, they spoke of advisors who were unconcerned with their needs, uninterested in students, unprepared to offer encouragement and support during the difficult dissertation years. In other words, while the American students interviewed complained about the lack of instrumental help from nominal advisors, foreign students missed both the instrumental and the expressive support that they felt should be forthcoming from a dissertation sponsor.

That foreign students look to their sponsor for encouragement and support as well as for substantive help is not surprising. During the predissertation years, this was also the case. American students were rather matter-of-fact, while foreign students tended to be quite distressed by perceived faculty neglect during the years prior to starting the thesis. Apparently, foreign students — particularly those from the Middle East and Latin America where faculty-student relationships are on a warmer, more informal footing — acutely resent the lack of such relationships during both the early and the later graduate years.

There is yet another factor which might account for the fact that foreign students were far less sanguine than Americans about the nominal supervisor: they were less likely to find emotional support from other sources. Recall, that one-half of the American students, but just one in three foreign students, were married at the time that they were writing their dissertations. And research suggests that the spouse is a critical source of emotional support for the graduate student, particularly during the stressful thesis years (Madrey, 1983). Further, foreign students were far less likely than their American counterparts to be part of mutual advising, peer support groups. Asian students, who tended to form their own peer networks, seemed less distressed than other foreign students about the lack of encouragement and support from the nominal supervisor.

In sum, both American and foreign students were angry and resentful about nominal supervisors from whom they were receiving minimal substantive assistance and guidance. Foreign students, however, perhaps because they had few other sources of emotional support during this stressful period, were particularly troubled by the lack of warmth and encouragement from such advisors.

A final note: Several professors suggested that one of the functions of a mentor was to guide students into academia. In their view, students who were bound for positions in industry or government could not be ignored but could hardly become their mentees. Faculty in the two engineering departments were particularly likely to note that mentorship was unlikely to develop because most students were headed for the more lucrative positions in industry rather than for academia. It is interesting to note, therefore, that there is a very strong correlation between a particular student's perception of his advisor and that student's plans after completing the dissertation. Every advisee, with no exception, who saw the advisor either as mentor or conscientious supervisor was headed for an academic career. In contrast, of the nine students who described their advisors merely nominal, all were either planning a career outside of the university or still were not certain about their plans.

Clearly then, the advisor/advisee relationship is significant not only for accomplishing the task at hand without undue stress, but it also has implications for the future career of the doctoral student. Given a sponsor who serves as a role model, both as teacher and advisor, a student is likely to opt for an academic career. Given the opposite, an advisor who provides only minimal time and assistance, much less warmth, encouragement, or support, students are more likely to turn away from the university setting and seek a career elsewhere. Further, the advisor stands to gain or lose a potential disciple or colleague.

The next chapter addresses one further aspect of advising at the doctoral level, namely, mutual or peer advising among doctoral students.

7

Students as Advisors: Mutual Advising Among Peers

Both in the broad sense of socialization into a professional culture as well as in the narrower sense of the communication of knowledge and information, advising may take place not only in the context of the relationship between sponsor and doctoral student, but also in the interaction among graduate students. Graduate students are likely to depend on each other to find their way through the thickets of American academic culture and to deal with the anxieties that are perhaps endemic, as well as unique, to graduate education. Graduate study in the arts and sciences tends to involve the special stress of ill-defined and apparently limitless expectations. While faculty advisors can help students to set realistic limits to their work, faculty cannot readily share the anxiety felt by graduate students. Therefore, it may be peers, that is, fellow students, who can best empathize with, understand, and help one another.

For foreign students, particularly those accustomed to more rigidly-specified curricular requirements, the stress of ill-defined expectations may be even more acute. Thus, even more than American students, they may require and seek advice, information, and support from peers, as well as from their faculty advisors. Further, foreign graduate students, at least in this sample, are less likely to be married than are their American counterparts and research suggests that, for married students, the major source of emotional support to counter the stresses of graduate study is the spouse (Madrey, 1983). All the more reason then foreign students might look to peers for support.

We might expect, further, that the extent of mutual or peer advising would vary inversely with the perceived quality of faculty advising. This, however, was not found to be the case. In fact, if there was any trend at all, it was the reverse. In other words, students who were satisfied with the quality of their relationship with their advisor, who saw the advisor either as mentor or conscientious supervisor, tended to be pleased as well with the amount of peer advising in the department. In contrast, where advisors were seen as merely nominal and faculty were perceived as uninterested in students, the students were somewhat less likely to report that they were able to turn to peers for advice and support.

For example, in the engineering department where students worked as a group, together with several professors, almost all were quite positive about the extent and quality of student interaction. As a Pakistani student put it:

> Yes — there's lots of mutual advising because we're working as a group and we see each other every day. Some of us are better than others in one or another area, so we can benefit from each other. We talk a lot with each other and I know that it helps me to be aware of just what they are doing and how. I hope it helps them.

The American student in the group felt that indeed it helped her:

> There's a lot of student-to-student communication here and I think it's great. [I'm even learning Chinese!] We get a good deal of substantive help from one another and sometimes it can save you time. For example, someone else may have an idea that he's abandoned because it didn't work out, so you know not to go up that alley.

In contrast, in the less prestigious engineering department where complaints about nominal advisors had prevailed, some students, at the least, tended to be dubious as well about the extent of peer support and help. A Lebanese student said:

> Peer advising? Not at all. There's no such thing as teams or groups of students here. You work alone. The students who have jobs in industry are lucky because they have people they can talk to and get help from.

An Asian student in the department also noted that he had no one to turn to although he recognized that this was not the case for all other students:

> Graduate students do help each other here, but there is no one in the lab who comes from my country, so I really don't have anyone I can talk to. I just come and go to the lab and that's it.

An American student in the department explained:

> There's some mutual advising, but it's basically only among close friends — I guess you could say cliques. I'm lucky — I have two other people and we read each other's material and bounce off ideas. I notice that the Korean students will get together to study for exams. They have a community, just of each other, directed toward passing courses and doing well. But if you're a foreign student with no one from your country, I guess you're in trouble.

Recall that students in the more highly rated economics department were, on the whole, dissatisfied with the quality of advising. They tended to see their sponsors as supervisors in name only and faculty, in general, as distant and uninvolved with students. Under such circumstances, we might expect a high rate of mutual advising among peers. Only one student, however, (an American) said that he had found peers helpful, particularly given the absence of input from his sponsor. He also reported the tendency for Korean students to form their own little support groups:

> Oh, yes. I don't know if there's much of it [mutual advising] in this department, but *I've* learned a lot from other students. I'd say that's the only thing that's gotten me through this whole thing, because I certainly didn't get it from faculty. For example, before giving a seminar paper, I'd try it out on friends. Also, some of us would read each other's chapters as we finished them. I don't know about other students, although I'd say that the Koreans, who have a lot of problems because of language, tend to get pushed into their own little clique.

The foreign students in this department, however, were virtually unanimous in their opinion that mutual advising among students was not too common. They attributed this largely to the competition among students for scarce departmental funds. Said a Chilean student:

> Everyone is competing for fellowship money and it's tough to make friends. It's very hard to develop relations with students here. People in economics are tough, very competitive. Frankly, you don't want to talk too much about what you're doing because you have to worry that they might steal your ideas.

A young woman from Argentina agreed although she also noted the tendency of Asians to form their own groups:

> There's very little mutual advising here because it's hard to develop relations with students. There's a lot of competition for money and this hurts relations. In addition, there's been a large erosion in the department and the good students who are left tend to go off by themselves. The only group of students where you have mutual support are the Asians because they need it so badly. The professors really ignore them, never read their stuff.

In the history department at this same university, the story was quite different. All students interviewed said that mutual advising among peers was not only common, but beneficial as well. In this department, as in economics, students had been more likely than not to describe their sponsors as merely nominal. However, unlike the economics students, those in history seemed to constitute a more cohesive group. An American student in Russian History, for example, said:

> We've got a lot of that [mutual advising]. People in Russian History tend to be a very tight group and fortunately, at my level there were enough of us, so I got a lot of advice, mostly about the 'hidden curriculum.' I mean things like what I should propose to read for Orals; just what Orals are like; personal dynamics in the department. And foreign students are part of the gang — definitely part of the student network. But they're mostly Mid-European; I don't know about students from Asia or the Middle East.

A student from the Middle East — an Israeli — was most emphatic about the importance of student networks, particularly in matters pertaining to the "hidden curriculum:"

> All the time I learn more from students probably than from my professors. Everything about how the system works. There's a network in the department and you hear about all kinds of things through this network. For example, you definitely learn about Orals from students — we have small study groups that prepare together. You also learn about how different faculty see things, which professors give you trouble, how the department works, how to get teaching jobs later.

An American student noted, however, that "plugging in" to an effective student group requires the kind of initiative and know-how that foreign students may lack:

> Oh yes — in every sense we have mutual advising among students. We set up miniseminars where we read each others stuff, and criticize each others work. After a while, *if they have any initiative*, some foreign students get plugged in. But those

who come from a really traditional society, such as Asians, tend to set up their own network.

Students in the history and economics departments at the other university were overall quite positive in their appraisals of their dissertation sponsors. In fact, none was described as a nominal supervisor and more students than not had perceived their thesis advisor as a mentor. Under such conditions, mutual advising among students might be unnecessary or minimal. We find, however, that just the reverse obtains. With the exception of one student from Iran, every other respondent spoke of the presence and importance of peer networks for mutual advising. And interestingly, this one exception is perhaps testimony to the fact that the major function of student networks is played out in the early years of the doctoral program when students are uncertain about such matters as requirements or about which professors to take and which to avoid. He said:

> I came in with a Masters and only needed 40 credits to finish. I knew just which courses I needed to round out my knowledge. I didn't need other students to tell me. In fact, I found that students tend to misguide you. For example, they make a very big deal over comprehensives and, as a result, I studied much too hard and much too long for them. Also, I heard a lot of very discouraging talk about how hard the dissertation is. I won't say it's easy, but they really overdo it.

For every other student, however, peer groups served a positive function. An American woman, in history, said:

> I've counted a lot on other students — peer counseling — for things like what classes to take, how to approach whom for money, who's in a good mood or a bad mood today. But foreign students, especially the Chinese, tend to have their own community of students from their country.

A Chinese student confirmed this observation:

Yes, there's a lot of students helping each other. About things likwe which courses are good and which aren't. During my first two years, I used to ask American students in my classes to check my papers for English. But it's mostly my Chinese friends that I talk with about ideas. In fact, it was in talking with them about different ideas that I came up with the topic I'm working on. I guess you tend to stick to your Chinese friends, Chinese movies, Chinese food.

Students' comments about mutual advising among peers suggest several conclusions. First, it appears that such advising is largely restricted to the predissertation years and focuses primarily on exchange of information about courses, professors, orals or comprehensives, or sources of fellowship monies. From the time that students settled in, for better or for worse, with a topic and an advisor, it was pretty much a "go-it-alone" proposition with the exception of those engineering students who were working daily with classmates on related projects. Students who were engaged in the process of writing their dissertations rarely asked (or were asked by) other students to comment on chapters, suggest avenues of research, or advise on how to proceed. This kind of guidance or assistance was expected of the thesis advisor; if it was not forthcoming, the student did not expect peers to fill the gap.

This suggests a second and related conclusion. Mutual student advising does not serve as an alternative to poor sponsor advising. Several students said they occasionally spoke with peers about dissertation-related questions and problems but with only one exception: these were candidates who were perfectly satisfied with the help and attention they were receiving from their sponsor. On the other hand, only one of the nine students who had characterized the sponsor as a nominal supervisor said that he had turned to fellow students for advice during the dissertation stage. All the others felt either that peers could not really be of help in this respect or, as several suggested, that the competitive ambiance of the department made students reluctant to help one another. Thus, in most instances students with nominal sponsors were doubly deprived: they received inadequate help from their advisor and at the same time were unable to turn to peers for assistance.

The data suggest yet a third conclusion about mutual advising among peers. Foreign students are considerably less likely than Americans to be part of an informal student network or clique that studies together, exchanges information, and serves in general as a support group. All but two of the Americans, but just one in three foreign students, said that they were part of such a network. One of the latter, an Asian student, mentioned that his network was comprised of students from his home country and, in fact, both foreign and American students in five of the six departments studied testified that Asian students tended to form their own study groups and cliques. The exception was the engineering department where the overwhelming majority of students were foreign and where students worked in a group on related projects, thus forming a natural cadre for mutual assistance.

We have seen in earlier sections that foreign students tend to enter the university with handicaps, compared to their American counterparts. They often come from educational institutions where curricular requirements are likely to be more rigidly structured; they don't know their way around the bureaucracy of the American university; they are hesitant to socialize with other students or to approach professors because of difficulty communicating in English. It is thus understandable that they either restrict their interaction to students from their home country or remain relatively isolated. In any event, they are less likely than the more gregarious, informal American students to reap the benefit of mutual peer advising and, accordingly, less likely to get to know which professors or courses to take and which to avoid, how to study for orals or comprehensives, which faculty members might be good thesis sponsors. Thus, the foreign student enters the dissertation stage with yet another handicap compared to the American student.

In the next and final chapter, we summarize some of the

differences that we have found between American and foreign doctoral students, differences that may appear early in the predissertation years but which help to explain why the advisor/advisee relationship itself may be more problematic for foreign than for American graduate students.

8
Foreign and American Doctoral Students: Conclusions and Recommendations

Before presenting several specific recommendations, we first summarize some of the major findings of this research, particularly those which relate to the foreign graduate student. We have found that the graduate years in general and the dissertation years in particular can indeed be stressful for both American and foreign doctoral students. For the most part, however, the predissertation years are relatively less stressful than the dissertation years that follow. There is a structure and a rhythm to these years which makes for a degree of security and predictability for students. They take some prescribed courses, study for examinations, write papers, serve as teaching or research assistants, prepare for orals or comprehensives. True, departmental offerings may be seen as skimpy and courses that are offered as unsatisfactory; requirements may be seen as unclear; orals or comprehensives may present stumbling-blocks; professors may be perceived as oblivious to the needs of students. Still, compared to the years that follow, the predissertation years present far fewer problems for the doctoral student.

Even during these years, however, foreign graduate students are likely to be at somewhat of a disadvantage compared to their American counterparts. They are older yet less likely to have the support of a spouse or other family member. They often enter with severe language handicaps which make them reluctant to speak up in classes and slower to complete assigned readings and papers. Some (Latin Americans and Israelis) are accustomed to interacting with professors on a fairly informal basis and are thus disappointed to find American faculty more aloof. Others — Asians in particular — have been taught to see faculty as authoritarian figures and to treat them with the greatest awe and respect; thus, they are hesitant to argue a point or to try to strike up an after-class relationship with professors. Perhaps as a result of these variations from American norms, Asians were perceived by faculty as overly dependent and lacking initiative, while Latin Americans and Israelis were sometimes described as overly aggressive and demanding. Language handicaps also deprive some foreign students both of the visibility and the valuable experience of the teaching assistantship. With minimal participation in mutual peer advising networks, they tend to look for professors not only for instrumental help, but also for emotional support and encouragement. Accordingly, they are particularly disappointed when these are not forthcoming.

Once coursework and comprehensives or orals, are completed doctoral students face the more difficult tasks of deciding upon a dissertation topic, searching for a thesis sponsor, struggling to convert an amorphous idea into a researchable topic, then actually writing the dissertation. During these years, students are basically on their own and must exercise considerable initiative and self-motivation to keep moving toward the goal of completing the thesis. And it is during these years, too, that structural constraints characteristic of a department combine with cultural handicaps endemic in some subgroups of foreign students to make this period particularly stressful for the latter. Lowered visibility during the predissertation years; relative isolation from effective peer networks; cultural traditions that dampen initiative; academic preparation that emphasizes knowledge-absorption rather than problem-solving — all of these may handicap foreign students as they seek a thesis advisor and engage in the difficult task of defining a research topic.

It is important to avoid the temptation, however, of adopting a "blame-the-victim" explanation for the academic or personal difficulties encountered by students, especially foreign students, lest we be diverted from some of the structural or institutional causes of these problems. Blaming the cultural "deficits" of foreign students simply deflects attention from possible institutional inadequacies. Thus, insufficient faculty in some areas of specialization; unduly heavy advisement loads; publication pressures; lack of peer recognition or reward for serving as thesis sponsor; outside consulting commitments — all of these lead many professors to define a good advisee as a student who requires a minimum of advising.

It appears then that institutional and cultural factors combine to create a situation where the qualities that advisors look for in advisees — the ability to come up with a well-defined topic, with the initiative to pursue an idea on their own, with well-developed research and writing skills — are the very qualities that foreign students, particularly Asians, are less likely than Americans to possess. Thus advisor expectations and advisee needs are less likely to mesh in the case of the foreign student.

This is not to say that American doctoral students do not find the dissertation years in general and the relationship with the sponsor in particular, problematic. As we have seen, however, American students often have other resources that foreign students lack. They can turn to other faculty or peers for instrumental help and to family and friends for emotional suppport.

Many foreign students plan, at least within a few years after obtaining the doctorate, to return to their home countries. Some will go back with very positive feelings about the years spent in graduate study and about the faculty who guided them in the dissertation period. Others will return with a degree of cynicism about the American system of graduate education, and with a particularly negative picture of faculty who give short shrift to the concerns of students and who provide little guidance and input into that major endeavor of the graduate years — the dissertation.

While this study cannot possibly attempt to generalize the experiences of all American and foreign doctoral students, it has pointed to some of the factors, both structural and psychological, that may make this experience a more or a less positive one. Hopefully, increased understanding of the conditions which are conducive to more satisfactory academic experiences for the most advanced graduate students — both foreign and American — will permit the avoidance of at least a limited number of frustrating experiences in the future.

RECOMMENDATIONS

I. Language handicaps

Finding:

Language handicaps have severe and continuing consequences for many foreign students, particularly those seeking doctorates in the social sciences and humanities.

Recommendation:

More thought and attention should be paid to setting realistic requirements in English proficiency and in providing adequate preparation to enable foreign students to meet these requirements.

2. Affective needs

Finding:

a. Foreign students often lack family and close friends who might be sources of support and encouragement during the graduate years. Further, they are less likely than Americans to be part of effective mutual advising peer networks.

b. Foreign student offices largely serve undergraduate foreign students, particularly in the area of hospitality programs, "surrogate family" programs, and the like.

Recommendations:
a. Departments might consider setting up a formal student advisory system. That is, each entering graduate student would be provided with a "buddy" or "big brother" who has already completed the coursework and entered the dissertation stage. Some universities have done this and have found that — if advisors are well-trained — peer advisory systems can work well (Fondacaro at al.,1984).

b. Special "outreach" efforts towards foreign graduate students should be undertaken, so that they too might benefit from the various hospitality programs that are sponsored by the foreign student office.

3.   Cultural differences

Finding:
Most professors give little thought to the question of differences between American and foreign students, particularly with respect to advising. Yet most acknowledge that there are indeed differences that impinge on the advisor/ advisee relationship.

Recommendations:
a. Departmental agendas should include alerting faculty to the fact that a number of students are coming from outside the United States and that the needs and expectations of many of these students may often be different from those of American students.

b. A representative of the foreign student office might be invited to attend a departmental meeting once every year or two to discuss specific problems or needs that foreign graduate students might present during the predissertation years and during the thesis stage.

c. The foreign student office might consider sponsoring a mini-conference (perhaps one-half day) each year for entering foreign graduate students and graduate departmental representatives. Topics would include differences in educational structures and norms; pitfalls and problem areas in graduate study; expectations and role relations, etc.

4.   The lack of reward for advising

Findings:
Advising in general, and dissertation sponsorship in particular, are not high priorities on professors' agendas. Nor are there any rewards or recognition offered for such advising. As a result, students —both American and foreign — are frequently short-changed. At the same time, this study as well as previous research suggest that the quality of the advisor/advisee relationship has important functions for both parties during and even after the dissertation stage.

Recommendation:
In some way, advising — particularly thesis advising — must be given higher priority within departments. Perhaps professors with more advisees might be given a lighter teaching load or even added compensation.

Appendix
The Foreign Student
Office

Can the Foreign Student Office serve as an alternative source of support for those students who may find it difficult to become part of a peer network or who may be unable to obtain satisfactory guidance from faculty advisors or dissertation sponsors? At each of the four university research sites, I spoke with the director of the Foreign Student Office in order to obtain an overview of the universities' policies and procedures for advising and counseling foreign students. In addition, I asked each foreign student advisee about the extent and nature of his or her contact with the Foreign Student Office.

At the beginning of each year, foreign students are generally expected to attend a one- or two-day orientation program. They receive maps of the city, together with listings of restaurants, museums, theaters, and the like and are appraised of the special caution that might be taken, particularly after dark, when negotiating the city streets and transit system. Orientation also includes introduction to the university campus, its libraries, administrative offices, dining facilities, health services, etc. Foreign students are urged to make use of the Foreign Student Office staff when problems arise. On some campuses, students are provided with regular opportunity to socialize with other foreign students at a bi-weekly tea or a monthly Open House.

The primary role of the Foreign Student Office, according to the directors with whom I spoke, is to deal with two major areas: immigration questions and problems (e.g. helping students keep their papers up-to-date) and financial matters (which usually involve providing official statements of student status to home country sponsors).

All four directors noted, however, that in addition to financial and immigration matters, foreign students turn to them for help with a wide range of problems such as finding adequate housing, difficulties with a roommate, health problems, and even marital conflicts. As one director put it:

> Our office tends to be a clearing-house for all of the many anxieties and problems of foreign students. Sometimes they come in just because they're lonely. In a sense, we serve as parent-substitutes.

Still, all four directors agreed that the role of the Foreign Student Office does not extend to academic advising either at the undergraduate or graduate level. At one university, however, the director noted that if students come in with complaints about an academic advisor, the staff tries to be of help:

> Sometimes a student who has difficulty fitting in culturally may in some way, unwittingly, offend a professor. The professor then wants to drop the student as an advisee. Our role is to try to translate the student's problem to the professor, perhaps saying the same thing, but in different words.

At this same university, the director noted that her small office could not possibly handle all aspects of student advisement, especially academic advisement. They are trying, however, to develop a network of people — administrative assistants to the deans of the various schools — whom they are sensitizing to the needs and problems of foreign students. In fact, they have already held several workshops and training sessions to this effect and expect to expand these efforts.

For most of the foreign graduate students with whom I spoke, contact with the Foreign Student Office was minimal and, if possible, to be avoided. Said a student from Portugal:

> I only go there for administrative problems, like when I need an exchange permit in order to get some money out of my country. But dealing with them is very difficult — it's a big bureaucracy and they don't care.

An Israeli student was even more negative:

> I hate them! I try to have as little contact as possible with them. I'm afraid that they won't renew my visa if they find out that I'm in financial trouble. Better I should stay out of their way!

According to an Iranian student, there was a very simple reason why graduate students had only minimal contact with the Foreign Student Office:

> Graduate courses are mostly in the evening and the office is closed!

It appears that students take a relatively jaundiced view of the Foreign Student Office and hardly regard it as an effective source of either practical or emotional — much less academic —assistance. They know, of course, that the Foreign Student Office is there to provide routine services that are largely connected their status as foreign students. Yet my conversations with the directors of these offices suggest that they are genuinely aware of and concerned about the special needs and problems of the foreign student and that they are actively involved in trying to address these needs. More concerted efforts might be directed, however, to outreach measures which might make foreign students more aware of the many other ways in which the Foreign Student Office can meet their special needs.

References

Alleman, E. et al. 1984 "Enriching mentoring relationships." *Personnel and Guidance Journal* 59: 329-33.

Baird, L.L. 1969 " A study of the role relations of graduate students." *Journal of Educational Psychology* 60: 15-21.

Bargar, R.R. and Mayo-Chamberlain, J.1983   "Advisor and advisee issues in doctoral education." *Journal of Higher Education* 54: 407-432.

Becker, H. et al. 1961 *Boys in White*. Chicago: University of Chicago Press.

Berelson, B. 1960   *Graduate Education in the United States*. New York: McGraw-Hill.

Bess, J.L. 1978 " Anticipatory socialization of graduate students." *Research in Higher Education* 8: 289-317.

Casas, J.M. and Atkinson, D.R. 1981 "The Mexican-American in higher education." *Personnel and Guidance Journal* 59: 473-476.

Connell, R.W.1985 *How to Supervise a Ph. D.* Vestes 28:38-42.

Dadfar, S. and Friedlander, M.L. 1982 "Differential attitudes of international students toward seeking psychological help." *Journal of Counseling Psychology* 29: 335-38.

Dillard, J.M. and Chisolm, G.B. 1983" Counseling the international student in a multicultural context." *Journal of College Student Personnel* 24: 101-104.

Dillon, M.J. and Malott, R.W.1981 "Supervising masters theses and doctoral dissertations." *Teaching of Psychology 8*: 195-202.

Doty, G.H.1962 An Appraisal of the Program Leading to the Doctor of Education Degree at Indiana University, Based on a Follow-up Study of its Graduates. Unpublished doctoral dissertation, Indiana University. Dissertation Abstracts 23:3792.

Fondacaro, M.R., Heller, K. and Reilly, M.J. 1984 "Development of friendship networks as a prevention strategy in a university megadorm." *Personnel and Guidance Journal* 62: 520-523.

Friedenberg, E.Z. and Roth, J.A. 1954 *Self-Perception in the University: A Study of Successful and Unsuccessful Graduate Students.* Chicago: University of Chicago Press.

Gollin, A. 1983 "The course of applied sociology: past and future." in H. E. Freeman et al.(eds.). *Applied Sociology: Roles and Activities of Sociologists in Diverse Settings.* San Francisco: Jossey-Bass.

Gottlieb, D. 1961 "Processes of socialization in American graduate schools." *Social Forces* 40: 124-131.

Heiss, A.M.1967 "Berkeley doctoral students appraise their academic programs." *Educational Record* 48: 30-44.

Jacks, P. et al.1983 "The ABCs of ABDs: a study of incomplete doctorates." *Improving College and University Teaching* 31: 74-81.

Jones, et al.(eds.) 1982 *An Assessment of Research Doctorate Programs in the United States.* Washington, D.C.: National Academy Press.

Kishkunas, L.J. 1958 A Study of Teachers College Doctoral Graduates Majoring in Administration and their Professional Preparation Programs. Unpublished doctoral dissertation, Teachers College, Columbia University.

Kozloff, J. 1984 "Recognition and reward of faculty advisors." Paper presented at the Annual Meeting of the National Conference on Academic Advising, Philadelphia, PA: 17pp.

Lafferty, S.1986 "Dissertations distinguish the graduate experience," *Columbia Daily Spectator,* February 27: 2.

Larsen, M.D.1983 "Rewards for academic advising: an evaluation." *NACADA Journal* 3: 53-60.

LeBaron,C. 1982 *Gentle Vengeance: An account of the first year at Harvard Medical School.* New York: Penguin.

Levinson, D.1978   *The Seasons of a Man's Life.* New York: Knopf.

Light, D. 1980 *Becoming Psychiatrists.* New York: Norton.

Loewenberg, P. 1969 "Emotional problems of graduate education." *Journal of Higher Education* 40: 610-23.

Madrey, F.C. 1983 "The effects of enrollment on full-time married doctoral students: an ethnographic study." Paper presented at Annual Meeting of Association for the Study of Higher Education, Washington, D.C.: 67 pp.

Mahdi, A. et al.1986 "Problems foreign students face as teaching assistants." American Sociological Association, Footnotes (December): 10.

Merton, R.K. et al.,eds.1957 *The Student-Physician.* Cambridge: Harvard University Press.

Nelson, R.L.1959 "Psychiatric needs of graduate students." *The School Review* 67: 93-105.

Page, J.V. 1959 Women and the Doctorate at Teachers College, Columbia University" . Unpublished doctoral dissertation, Teachers College, Columbia University.

Persell, C. 1976 *Quality, Careers and Training in Educational and Social Research.* Bayside, N.Y.: General Hall Publishers.

Raines, H.1986 "A mentor's presence." *The New York Times Magazine,* July 20: 46.

Rasky, S.F. 1985 "They labor in foothalls of academe." *The New York Times,* June 12: C16.

Renetzky, A. 1966 All But the Dissertation: A Study of the Factors of Attrition in Graduate Education. Unpublished doctoral dissertation, University of Southern California: Dissertation Abstracts, 29:1405-A.

Reskin, B.F. 1979 "Academic sponsorship and scientists' careers." *Sociology of Education* 52: 129-146.

Rosen, B.C. and Bates, A.P.1967 "The structure of socialization in graduate school." *Sociological Inquiry* 37: 71-84.

Rosenhaupt, H. 1958 *Graduate Students' Experience at Columbia University* 1940-1956. New York: Columbia University Press.

Solmon, L.C. and Beddow, R. 1984 "Flows, costs, and benefits of foreign students to the United States: Do we have a problem?" in E. Barber, ed. *Foreign Student Flows* , Institute of International Education

Sorenson, G. and Kagan, D.1967 "Conflicts between doctoral candidates and their sponsors." *Journal of Higher Education* 38: 17-24.

Strom, L.E. 1965 "Some personality dimensions of doctors of education." *Journal of Experimental Education* 33: 387-90.

Turner, R.F. 1972 The doctoral dissertation sponsor: a study of role expectations. Unpublished doctoral dissertation, Teachers College, Columbia University.

Turow, S.1977 *One L.* New York: Penguin.

Valdez, R. 1982 "First year doctoral students and stress." *College Student Journal* 16:30-37.

Van Maanen, J.V. 1983 " Golden passports: managerial socialization and graduate education.*" Review of Higher Education* 5: 435-455.

Walter, L.M. 1982 "Lifeline to the underprepared." *Improving College and University Teaching* 30: 159-163.

Wright, C.R. 1964 "Success or failure in earning graduate degrees." *Sociology of Education* 38: 73-97.

Zuckerman, H. 1977 *Scientific Elite: Nobel Laureates in the United States*. New York: Free Press.

IIE RESEARCH SERIES

Readers of this IIE Research Report may be interested in earlier titles in the series. They are available through the Educational Resources Information Center (ERIC) Clearinghouse on Higher Education, One Dupont Circle, NW, 630, Washington DC 20036-1183.

Report #1
ABSENCE OF DECISION:
Foreign Students in American Colleges and Universities
Craufurd D. Goodwin
Michael Nacht

Report #2
BLACK EDUCATION IN SOUTH AFRICA:
The Current Situation
David Smock

Report #3
A SURVEY OF POLICY CHANGES:
Foreign Students in Public Institutions of Higher Education
Elinor G. Barber

Report #4
THE ITT INTERNATIONAL FELLOWSHIP PROGRAM :
An Assessment After Ten Years
Maranthi Zikopoulous
Elinor G. Barber

Report #6
INTERNATIONAL EXPERTISE IN AMERICAN BUSINESS:
How to Learn to Play with the Kids on the Street
Stephen J. Kobrin

Report #7
FOREIGN STUDENT FLOWS:
Their Significance for American Higher Education
Elinor G. Barber, Editor

Report #8
A SURVEY OF POLICY CHANGES:
Foreign Students in Public Institutions of Higher Education 1983- 1985
William Mc Cann Jr.

Report #9
DECLINE AND RENEWAL:
Causes and Cures of Decay Among Foreign-Trained Intellectuals and
Professionals in the Third World
Craufurd D. Goodwin
MIchael Nacht

Report #10
CHOOSING SCHOOLS FROM AFAR:
The Selection of Colleges and Universities in the United States By Foreign
Students
Maranthi Zikopoulous
Elinor G. Barber

Report #11
THE ECONOMICS OF FOREIGN STUDENTS
Stephen P. Dresch

Report #12
THE FOREIGN STUDENT FACTOR:
Their Impact on American Higher Education
Lewis C. Solmon
Betty J. Young

Report #13
INTERNATIONAL EXCHANGE OFF- CAMPUS:
Foreign Students and Local Communities
Mark Baldassare
Cheryl Katz